Ekaterina Filatov

UNDERSTANDING THE PEOPLE AROUND YOU:

AN INTRODUCTION TO SOCIONICS

UNDERSTANDING
THE PEOPLE AROUND YOU:
AN INTRODUCTION TO SOCIONICS

For information, contact:
MSI Press
1760-F Airline Highway, #203
Hollister, CA 95023

Library of Congress Control Number 2004102209

ISBN 978-0-9679907-6-7

cover design by CDL Services

Printed in the United States of America

CONTENTS

FOREWARD   5

PREFACE   7

ACKNOWLEDGMENT   10

INTRODUCTION   11

Part I. **THE BASIS OF SOCIONICS — JUNGIAN FUNCTIONS**   17

   THINKING VS. FEELING, SENSING VS. INTUITION   17

   STATE OF MIND (Attitude): EXTRAVERTED VS. INTROVERTED TYPES   21

   SYMBOLS OF JUNGIAN FUNCTIONS   23

   PERSONALITY PROGRAM DETERMINED BY EACH JUNGIAN FUNCTION .   24

   LEADING BLOCK OF A PSYCHOLOGICAL TYPE   27

   THE OCCUPATIONAL MINDSETS   29

   JUNGIAN MODEL (The Model J)   33

   RATIONALITY VS. IRRATIONALITY   36

Part II. **PSYCHOLOGICAL TYPES**   39

   TEMPORAL INTUITION: ROMANTIC AND CRITIC   44

   SELF-PERCEPTIVE SENSING: EPICUREAN AND CRAFTSMAN   51

   RELATIONAL FEELING: PSYHOLOGIST AND GUARDIAN   59

   STRUCTURAL THINKING: ANALYST AND STRUCTURIST   68

   POTENTIALITY INTUITION: INITIATOR AND SEEKER   76

   VOLITIONAL SENSING: LEADER AND ORGANIZER   84

   EMOTIONAL FEELING: PERFORMER AND ENTHUSIAST   92

   PRACTICAL THINKING: PROFESSIONAL AND ENTERPRISER   101

Contents

Part III. **INTERTYPE RELATIONSHIPS** 110

   1. DUALITY RELATIONSHIP (Mutual Complementain) 113

   2. SEMI-DUALITY RELATIONSHIP (Incomplete Complementation) 119

   3. CONTRASTIVE RELATIONSHIP 120

   4. ILLUSIONARY RELATIONSHIP 121

   5. MIRROR RELATIONSHIP 122

   6. CONFLICTIVE RELATIONSHIP 123

   7, 8. RELATIONSHIP OF SUPERVISION 124

   9. RELATIONSHIP OF IDENTITY 129

   10. KINDRED RELATIONSHIP 130

   11. SUPER-EGO RELATIONSHIP 131

   12. COLLABORATION RELATIONSHIP 132

   13. RELATIONSHIP OF ACTIVATION 132

   14. RELATIONSHIP OF QUASI-IDENTITY 133

   15, 16. RELATIONSHIP OF SOCIAL REQUEST 134

   MORE ABOUT THE RELATIONSHIPS 136

CONCLUDING REMARKS 159

Appendix I. **Analysis of Psychological Peculiarities of the Heroes of M. Mitchell's** *Gone With The Wind* **And Their Relations From The Socionic Standpoint.** 144

Appendix II. **Test** 159

Literature 167

Internet 168

FOREWARD

I am honored to have the opportunity to introduce Dr. Ekaterina Filatova's research and theories to the English-speaking public and to have been a small part of it being published in the United States. She was one of the first people to write about socionics and has gathered a large and loyal following in Russia and the countries of the former Soviet Union.

I first met Dr. Filatova in the early years of this century. At the time, I was heavily involved in applying the theories and research of Jungian psychology to the teaching of foreign languages—actually, to the teaching of any K-16 subject—and had both lectured and written extensively about it before being introduced to Dr. Filatova on one of my lecture trips to St. Petersburg by Dr. Dmitry Lytov, then a professor of psychology (and translator of one of my books). An ardent practitioner of socionics, Dr. Lytov and I had frequently discussed the differences between socionics, the system of Jungian psychology developed in Eastern Europe and the Myers-Briggs Type Indicator, the system of Jungian psychology used in the United States. I quickly saw that the Eastern European socionics approach to the application of Jung's theories to various psychological situations in life (e.g., forming relationships) more closely followed the original descriptions of Jung than did the MBTI system spread by then throughout the United States.

Dr. Filatova had published a number of notable works by the time I met her, and she had become widely known and respected in Russia as one of the leaders, if not the most significant leader, of the socionics movement. Her works were seminal in many respects. I believed that they would be of great interest and use to American readers, but, unfortunately, they were available only in Russian, which I could read but had no time to translate.

Thus arose the idea to present Dr. Filatova's works to the West, hopefully as the seminal publication here, as well as in the East. Not having run into anyone else of any consequence or with the extent of theoretical and research knowledge of Dr. Filatova in the intervening years, I have the courage to declare here that this book can be considered a seminal publication in what I hope will become the field of American socionics, centering around Dr. Filatova's work.

I urge those who work in the area of MBTI and therefore are well acquainted with the works of Jung to explore how Dr. Filatova, representing the approach of those in the socionics movement throughout Europe, has organized Jungian theory into a system that both parallels and diverges from MBTI and to compare socionics and MBTI. It may be that you will change your allegiance, and even if not, Dr. Filatova will surely bring some additional insights into your understanding of Jungian psychology. I would have used these introductory pages to make an in-depth comparison of the two systems, but it has been several years now since I have worked in this field—life has a way of moving us on into areas with which we had not expected to be associated. In any event, MBTI practitioners will quickly see those differences, as I did when I first became associated with socionists.

This book has been several years in the making. I think both Dr. Filatova and I began to despair of it ever seeing the light of day, considering a collaboration that spanned the Atlantic Ocean, another whole continent, and eleven time zones. Our efforts, though—and I have to admit that her efforts were by far the greatest—have resulted in a gem of a work for the American reading public. I believe that any parent, any spouse, any teacher, any student, any counselor, any employer, any employee, and indeed anyone with or desiring friends will find insights in this book that will help him or her truly understand the people around him or her in ways that will forever change his or her life for the better.

You may not know it now, but you hold a treasure in your hands. Once you have finished reading it, you will know it for certain!

Betty Lou Leaver, PhD

PREFACE

The modern man is a communicator. Every day we come in contact with dozens, sometimes even hundreds of people, from our friends to complete strangers. The efficiency of our business, as well as our social authority, leisure satisfaction, comfort and relaxation at home depend on our ability to communicate with business partners, colleagues, friends, relatives and just casual acquaintances. I would even prefer to say «the art of communication» instead of «ability to communicate», because true communication is a creative act rather than a craft skill. One can master rules of courtesy, but they are not enough to understand people's motivation, to predict their reaction to our words and deeds. Too often we presume that other people would act in the same way as we do. Sadly, very often such presumptions result in frustration and disappointment. Other people's souls are often hidden in «darkness». Is it really possible to communicate with such «dark shadows»? How nice would it be to dissipate the mysterious darkness and to find a road map! Not too long ago there was no such map; now it's available! A new science of interpersonal communication called Socionics offers us such a road map.

According to scientific tradition, communication is considered a subject of psychology. Social psychologists pay especially great attention to this subject. They have published large monographs, numerous manuals, hundreds of articles dedicated to problems of human communication; however, they wisely suspended direct advice, strict classifications, and algorithms of communication activities. For them, communication remains *terra incognita*, just like thinking, memory, and conscience. The young science Socionics was created not by professional psychologists, but by economists, mathematicians, and physicists who think in terms of models and theories, not single facts. The result is an interesting scientific hybrid — a traditional Humanitarian subject researched by scientific methods. The hybrid proved to be not only viable but very productive as well. I believe that socionic formulae and schemes have the same meaning for human studies as the Periodical Table for chemistry.

However, it would be wrong to say that Socionics rejects the scientific background of the classical psychology. On the contrary, Socionics uses it in the most rational way.

The starting point of the socionic theory is the fundamental psychological typology proposed by Carl Gustav Jung, an established authority of 20th century psychology. In Socionics Jung's ideas acquire a rational and logical shape. The most important achievement of Socionics is its theory of intertype relationships. This theory is a real scientific discovery. Psychology has not known anything like that before. The intertype relationships determine the nature of interpersonal communication from aggressive and conflicting to peaceful and comfortable. By knowing your own psychological type and being capable of determining those of other people, by knowing how these types work together, you will be able to predict with whom you can or cannot easily get along. Young women who understand Socionics make correct choices of their partners to create happy families.

The author of this book Ekaterina Filatova is one of the pioneers of Socionics in Russia. She began her scientific career in physics, for many years she lectured in various fields of physics at several universities, and became an experienced and established university professor. Still, she felt that she was missing something really important in her professional self-fulfillment. She was introduced to Socionics in the late 1980s, and this acquaintance completely changed her life. Her intellectual, emotional, and moral potential found a great field of application. A university professor became a pioneer and discoverer of perspectives of a new science. Numerous experiments with participation of hundreds of enthusiastic students attracted by Filatova's lectures became sources of valuable socionic knowledge. Critical study of publications, discussions with colleagues, preparation and publication of six monographs in Socionics, as well, as multiple theoretical and popular scientific articles — this was Ekaterina Filatova's way toward the book you are holding in your hands.

This book is not a compilation of various authors' works but a complete study of a single author that is able to meet expectations of the most demanding reader. Ekaterina Filatova represents the humanistic trend in the modern Socionics. She treats Socionics as a science of understanding and agreement between people. For every human being, humanistic communication with other people is a true island of salvation in the cruel world of competition, uncertainty, threats, and stresses. For this reason, everybody needs Socionics. The modern human needs three kinds of literacy: orthographic literacy, computer literacy, and communicative literacy. Ekaterina Filatova's book is an excellent manual in communication addressed to people of all ages, occupations, and with different life experience.

Member of the Russian Academy
of Natural Sciences,
Professor A.V.Sokolov

A fragment from one of numerous letters received by the author after the first publication of this book:

«For many years, your book has been my only guide in the world of Socionics. My students read it until the pages fell apart, took the book home, meticulously repaired, and then read again. This particular copy of your book is worth registering as a Guinness record, since it was read by more than 1000 people! Your book undoubtedly helped many young people to find their ways in life».

Actor and teacher
Tatyana Men'shova

ACKNOWLEDGMENTS

This book could be published in English only due to efforts of several people who expressed their sincere desire to help spread socionic knowledge around the world.

It all began in 2003 when three individuals met in the Russian city of St. Petersburg: Betty Leaver, an American who displayed a keen interest in challenging scientific discoveries, especially in psychology and pedagogy; Dmitri Lytov, a Russian, translator and a psychologist interested in Socionics; and a former Russian and now American citizen, high school student Anna Ivanova, who at that time visited St. Petersburg with her parents.

Dmitri convinced Betty of the perspectives of publishing a socionic book in the United States, and Anna Ivanova offered herself as a translator. Anna translated several chapters (her parents had studied Socionics and assisted her in translation). Dmitri finished the translation, wrote some notes to the text, helped to verify terminology and proposed short lists of celebrities known in the West (originally the book contained lists of Russian celebrities).

I would also like to cordially thank a very nice couple, Tatiana and Mikhail Makarov from St. Petersburg who sponsored part of the translation.

My very special gratitude goes to Betty Leaver. Being educated in the former USSR, I used to perceive Americans as exceptionally pragmatic people who do everything for the sake of profit. Betty managed to break this prejudice. I really appreciate her wonderful altruism, her generosity and understanding. Sincerely willing to help, she assisted Anna in translation and did a great work of editing and preparing the book for publication. Dear Betty, without you this book would never be possible.

May, 2009
Ekaterina Filatova

INTRODUCTION

For centuries, despite multiple discoveries in the field of natural science, people still struggled to answer simple questions related to human nature and the laws of psychological compatibility. Since ancient times people understood the convenience of dividing people into several groups based on certain criteria. Each group would combine individuals with similar psychological traits radically different from traits in other groups. As a result, various typologies emerged with the purpose of creating generalized portraits of people belonging to different types. By now we know dozens of such typologies based on various parameters. This plethora of typologies leads to two conclusions:

— Typological approach has many advantages in understanding human nature and finds more and more supporters who continue looking for more effective ways to classify people according to their psyche;

— Researchers still cannot find a universal foundation allowing for precise and reliable description of behavioral traits of every individual; therefore the search is going on.

In view of these two facts I would like to present to the readers a new typology called Socionics.

The emergence of Socionics was preceded by an important discovery. Carl Gustav Jung (1875—1961) — a Swiss psychiatrist and the founder of analytical psychology suggested the typology based on four basic psychological functions in human psyche: thinking, feeling, sensation, and intuition. The result of many years of work describing the laws of behavior of these groups was Jung's book, *Psychological Types* published in 1924.

In 1979, a Lithuanian researcher, «a teacher by profession and a sociologist by interest», Aushra Augustinavichiute, returned to the theory of the great Swiss psychoanalyst. She came to the conclusion that a Jungian psychological type is an inborn psychological structure that delineates a specific nature of informational exchange between a person and his or her social environment. Based on Jung's typology, she developed rules, which not only describe the structure of a person's psyche, but also allow for determination of human interactions. Her work attracted enthusiasts of different ages and professions who also made their contributions to the development of this captivating field of knowledge. Involvement of people with education in the disciplines other than traditional psychology (natural science, mathematics, engineering, etc.) allowed for a new look at the problem of organization of human psyche. Moreover, besides establishing psychological types Socionics answered one of the most fundamental questions of practical psychology — it formulated the laws of interaction between representatives of different psychological types. The significance of this discovery can hardly be overestimated.

Therefore, the reader already understands that Socionics is about two main psychological problems: the research of typology, and the establishment of the laws behind the relations between various psychological types.

An important step in solving the first problem was the distinct identification of the eight Jungian functions— extraverted or introverted thinking, feeling, sensation, and intuition, — the eight fundamental elements determining human psyche. For example, one of the functions, extraverted sensation, is called **volitional sensing**, and characterized as: «Volitional pressuring, activeness, purposefulness, and spatial control». Another function, introverted feeling, is called **relational feeling**, and characterized as: «Adherence to moral issues, guarding of principles, and observance of traditions».

From these eight elements, socionics recognizes 16 versions of psychological structure were created which can actually be encountered in reality. In this way, it became possible to describe the fundamentals of each psychological type in a compact form.

Depending on the place, or **channel,** that a function occupies in the psyche's structure, it plays different roles. For example, if the function **volitional sensing** occupies the most powerful channel of the psyche, which is called the **personality program channel**, then the person whose psychological type is determined by this structure considers it most important that the world is ruled by force, and will act accordingly within the boundaries of their «force mentality». In a different structure the same function may reside in the weak area, the **vulnerable channel**, and for the owner of this structure, everything related to force, no matter what form it comes in, is the «greatest evil». These people see force as revolting, immoral, and intolerable, especially if they have the element **relational feeling** in their personality program channel.

Imagine that two people with the psychological types that are determined by the structures described above found themselves in the army. It is obvious that the first person is in their element; but for the second, being a soldier would be a source of constant stress, especially if it is necessary to shoot and kill. However, if these two people end up working as daycare providers, then the forceful methods employed by the first person will likely be out of place, while the second person could not find a better place to fulfill their strongest qualities.

Our physical qualities are apparent to everyone. For example, an undersized athlete understands perfectly that he or she is not likely to achieve astonishing success on a basketball court. Psychological traits, however, are not as apparent. Due to this, there are people around us who are unhappy with their chosen careers and feel that their «true calling» lies somewhere outside the boundaries of their profession. People worry and suffer because of this; sometimes their subconscious desolation may result in aggression aimed at surrounding people who seem to be living happier lives. This explains the importance for each individual to understand the strong and weak sides of their psychological structure.

Let us move on the second problem — the problem of interaction between representatives of different psychological types. «Hell is other people», Jean-Paul Sartre said. Such a harsh comment from the famous French philosopher has not yet been contested. Moreover, it is confirmed thousands of times daily. However, if agree that interaction between two people follows certain laws, then, by relying on these laws, «hell» could be avoided. Socionics is the science which describes those laws. Thus, Socionics gives people a reliable guide to relationships between different psychological types, and therefore helps to predict the consequences of human interactions.

In the previous example of two different psychological types, the function **volitional sensing** is situated in different channels — for one type it is in the strongest **personality program channel**, while for the other type it is in a rather weak channel called the **vulnerable channel**. It is obvious that any active, resolute, and obstinate behavior on the part of the first individual would cause extreme aggravation and unhappiness in the second; therefore, conflict is unavoidable.

Add to that pair a third individual for whom the function **volitional sensing** is located in the weakest, **suggestible channel**. This channel is organized in such a way that it constantly asks for help in its sphere of action. In this case, an individual delightedly hands over all the resolute action to his partner, content to «go with the flow» and submit to somebody. Thus, the third individual perceives the first individual as a willing helper and a leader upon whom all responsibility can be placed, and thereby receiving a feeling of safety and conformity in return.

What is happening here? The actions, statements, advice, and comments of one person (in the given situation, by the wielder of the strongest **volitional sensing** function) bring out entirely different reactions in two other people belonging to different psychological types. These resolute actions cause aggravation, distress and, possibly, aggression in the second person, while the third person has a sense of being cared for, a feeling of protection and psychological comfort.

There are 16 types of intertype relationships discovered and described in Socionics. Four intertype relationships belong to the comfort sphere, four to the strong discomfort sphere and the other eight are intermediate.

This kind of knowledge is absolutely invaluable to engaged couples, in the solutions of parent-child problems, and to teachers in developing potential abilities and adequate career orientation of their students.

It is also extremely important to consider the laws of psychological compatibility during the formation of any cooperative group. At school, it may happen that a teacher finds him or herself in a socionic conflict relationships with some of their students. Socionics may help to explain the reason why someone is getting low grades, disrupting the class, teasing and insulting other children, or starting fights. Socionics may also play an important role in business activities. Indeed, an appropriate hiring policy and teamwork chemistry will increase efficiency and thereby competitiveness of any business.

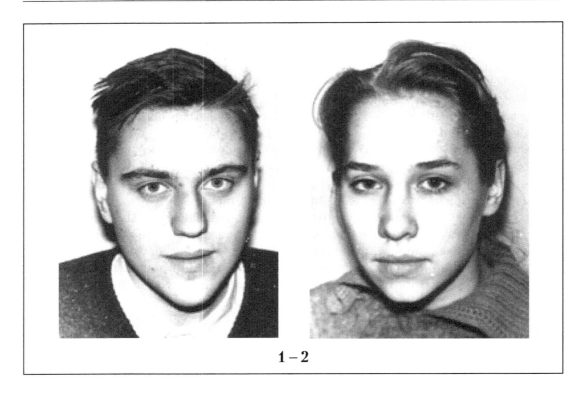

1 – 2

3 – 4

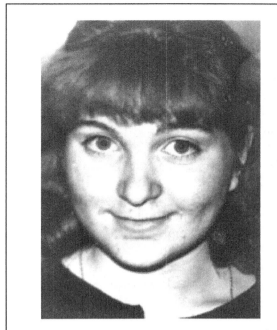 

5 – 6

7 – 8

Humans are social creatures, and Socionics has been successfully applied in all branches of human life, the reason being that the discipline of Socionics deals not only with individual typologies, but also with human interrelationships.

One question often emerges at introductory lectures in Socionics: what is the principal difference between Socionics and other typologies? Based on the fundamental principles formulated by Jung, Socionics builds a new model describing the structure of human psyche. In this model eight Jungian functions are considered as functions of an informational metabolism. Each function affects the psyche differently depending on the informational channel it occupies. Based on this model, Socionics formulated the laws of interaction of these functions in the human psyche and on this foundation described 16 principal types of interpersonal relationships, which are different from those suggested by other typologies.

Finally, take a good look at the pictures below. Let me point out in advance, that there is not a single pair of blood relatives among these people.

Yes, you are right — these are *doppelgangers*, each pair (1—2, 3—4, 5—6, 7—8) belongs to one of distinct psychological types:

   — the individuals in photographs 1 and 2 belong to the **Pragmatic** group;
   — those in photographs 3 and 4 belong to the **Researcher** group;
   — those in photographs 5 and 6 belong to the **Socialist** group;
   — those in photographs 7 and 8 belong to the **Humanist** group.

This is a purely experimental fact. Socionics has revealed the connection between human psyche and physical characteristics thus demonstrating the genetic determination of psychological traits. Not only twins but also unrelated people may be doppelgangers both in appearance and psychologically. Thus, we believe that Socionics has discovered an «elementary» type determined on the genetic level. This is another principal difference of Socionics from all other typologies. This issue is discussed in detail in the author's book *Personality in the Mirror of Socionics* which includes several hundred photographs of people belonging to different psychological types including around 100 of *doppelganger* pairs.

Part I
THE BASIS OF SOCIONICS —
JUNGIAN FUNCTIONS

Now we invite the reader to a more detailed acquaintance with this new exciting sphere of knowledge of human beings.

Logically, each social group needs to include specialized individuals, biologically preprogrammed for specialization in certain functions necessary for survival of this group. Reproduction, feeding, defense, strategy and tactics of behavior of a group, adaptation to new conditions — all these tasks should be performed by people naturally predetermined for fulfillment of specific tasks. Specialization is necessary, because it is socially justified.

How does this specialization work? It must be determined by neural processes, ways of reacting towards external irritants, or, technically speaking, by the structure of the human informational system. For humans it means certain choices of psychological characteristics that help them fulfill their social mission.

Thus we have to admit that human specialization has profound meaning: their very nature prevents people from being psychologically universal. Human psyche includes a system of filters that, on the one hand, eliminates unnecessary information, and on the other, focuses on certain kind of activity necessary to the society.

What are these filters? And how does the mechanism of the human psyche work? What are the directions in which it moves the mind? Socionics gives answers to these questions.

Thinking vs. Feeling, Sensation vs. Intuition

People are granted a variety of skills at different levels. Generally, one function is dominant in a person. In relation to these functions, four types can be identified: i) the thinking type; ii) the feeling type; iii) the sensing type; iv) the intuitive type. What are their general attributes?

The Thinking Type (Thinker) is a person for whom an objective world, a world of hierarchy and laws, dominates. These people's interests may be focused on the invention of new machines and mechanisms. They may be engrossed in the creation of scientific theories or deliberate on the structure of the universe, but rarely does the social world interest them.

For Thinkers, only proven facts can be used to support arguments. They do not allow themselves to take rash actions or make hasty statements, and if it happens, they consider it unacceptable. If it is impossible to get by without emotion, they use the socially accepted stereotypical way of showing emotions; they have a standard collection of gestures and smiles. If the situation is out of the ordinary, they experience confusion.

The Feeling Type (Feeler), contrary to the Thinker, is aimed towards relationships with others. These individuals tend not to get involved with scientific theories and constructions. They are more attracted to the questions of good and evil, love and hate, and ethical and moral problems. The Feeling type is easily influenced; the opinions of others can be weighty arguments in Feelers' decision making. This is especially true if the arguments are based on a logical reasoning. Feelers feel very insecure in the logical sphere and try to stick to the norms accepted by society in this issue.

In displaying their emotions, Feelers are, on the contrary, quite open, using a wide spectrum of emotional expressions. Due to this, they can easily and unerringly establish the correct psychological space when socializing: they focus on how people talk, what gestures they make, their facial expressions, poses, intonations, and the like.

Thinking and feeling abilities of a person are related conversely: a strong thinking psychological type is generally not very emotional, while a person of an extremely emotional feeling psychological type has only a slight grasp of the capabilities of the thinking type. Thus, we have a pair of opposites, which is recognized as the first dichotomy in Socionics.

Example: «Alex, don't you think that life in our class is boring: we do not visit with each other, do not meet in night clubs or parties, do not celebrate birthdays?..»

After some hesitation Alex replies: «You see, Irene, I don't. In fact I don't understand why people grouped together by occasion should spend time together».

Certainly, in this case Irene belongs to the feeling type and Alex to the thinking.

> **Thinkers** — *they focused on objective reality, objective regularities (such as the laws of physics, the processes of production), may display rigidity on behalf of a job, and value professionalism.*

> **Feelers** — *they are people of emotions, though do not necessarily display those emotions, depend on the opinion of others, easily get into emotional conflicts, able to establish adequate psychological distance.*

Let us move on to the next dichotomy.

The Sensing Type (Senser) characterizes people who live «in the here and now». Their attention is constantly focused on everything around them, their perception is exceptionally concrete, and they easily notice even the smallest changes in their surroundings. They are sensitive to comfort and coziness, which they are generally very good at creating, as they strive towards them.

It is easy for these people to switch their attention from any distress simply by changing their surroundings. It is hard for them to wait for prosperity to come. They need to get what they want immediately. Their motto is action. For the Senser, being able to quickly switch from one task to another, keep track of changes in their surroundings, and easily adapt to these changes is characteristic.

The Intuitive Type (Intuiter), as opposed to the sensing type, integrates personal impressions into images and symbols. Intuiters, while isolating themselves from distracting trivialities, can «see» the essence of processes or phenomena. Due to this trait, the outer manifestation is nothing but a nudge to awaken creativity and push them to craft new inventions or forecast the future. With equal ease, they travel back into the past, reliving it anew, as if the events of old occur again and again. In everyday life, they may seem absent-minded, as if they do not notice what is going on around them. Their thoughts wander, thus they quickly disconnect from first impressions. It is extremely hard for these kinds of people to carry out routine work because in every repetition of the same action they are tempted to bring something new to it, something different from the previous time, though this new idea might turn out be worse than the conventional old way.

For this reason, people of this type do not like to be responsible for providing comfort and convenience. It would not be right to say that they are indifferent to such matters, but sometimes they can neglect the disarray around them, being focused on their thoughts rather than on specific material things (the latter is rather characteristic of the sensing type).

Sometimes intuition is understood as a capability of good prediction of events, but this is not universally true. Sometimes a sensing type, especially a sensing-thinking one, can much better calculate the outcome of the events than an intuitive one. The people of intuitive type rather synthesize apprehensions in their conscience and thus can fail in their forecasts without good grasp of the real situation.

> *Example:* «*Dasha, bring me some cheese, it is on the top shelf in the fridge*», *a mother asks her daughter.*
>
> «*Mommy, I don't see any cheese inside!*» *Her mother, being well aware of her daughter's habits, comes to the kitchen herself and opens the fridge:* «*Here it is, right in front of you. How could you not find it?*»

In this situation, of course, the mother is of a sensing type and her daughter is intuitive.

Here, as with the Thinker and Feeler pair, we can see a reverse dependence. The Senser, whose attention is entirely taken up with material objects, is unlikely to spend great length of time on fantasies and dreams. The Intuiter, on the contrary, will not bother studying the details of the material world because impressions are more important for Intuiters than reality. Here we encounter the second dichotomy in Socionics. As in the Thinker-Feeler pair, a person can be either a Senser or an Intuiter.

> **Sensers** — *they view the world concretely and live «in the here and now». They value comfort and are able to create it. They strive towards practical action and prefer to receive the results of their work in material form.*

> **Intuiters** — *they are characterized by the perception of reality in its integrity. They are dreamers and romantics, experimentalists and generators of a multitude of ideas, often unfeasible. They might be absent-minded and prefer attractive but doubtful possibilities to real, dependable profit.*

We now have enough information to come to important conclusions.

Since the axes of Thinking/Feeling and Sensation/Intuition are independent, let us position them on a plane perpendicular to each other. We will then have four groups corresponding to four sections. Each of these groups is characterized by only two strong functions.

Table 1.1. **Socionic types by occupational mindsets**

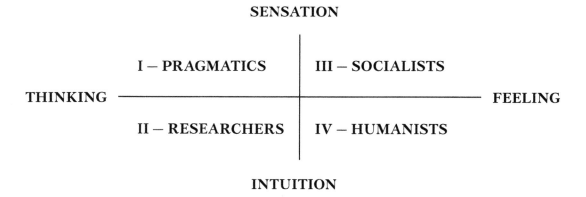

Here are some important conclusions:

I — PRAGMATICS have strong thinking and sensing; thinking makes them judicious, logical, and self-collected, while sensing makes their thinking thrifty and concrete.

Therefore, such people can make a good career for example in industry, construction, or agriculture. It is unlikely for Pragmatics to start an undertaking without being sure of a certain reward for their efforts.

II — RESEARCHERS have strong thinking and intuition. They are permanently in search of unusual solutions to various problems; their intuition helps them to easily generate ideas while thinking provides a method of rational implementation of these ideas. Such people are efficient in business, management, and science. For many Researchers truth is more important than immediate advantage.

III — SOCIALISTS have strong feeling and sensation. Sensation enables them to recognize their own physical needs and those of other people, while the feeling function represents fine tuning of their relations with people. These are Socialists in the broadest meaning of this word — doctors, social workers, restaurateurs, or people in show business. People of these occupations tend to value physical comfort and warmth of relations.

IV — HUMANISTS are the least practical of all types, nevertheless possessing their own strengths, namely feeling and intuition. They perceive other people's emotions, can relieve stress, create psychological comfort using their feeling function, while intuition makes them poetic, daydreaming, and often sublime. They are keepers of the spiritual world. Humanists are frequently encountered among actors, poets, artists, and religious leaders.

Even such short descriptions of the main occupational presets of the human psyche may be very useful. However, now we are going to consider dichotomies which will allow us to make even more precise differentiation within each of the four groups. The first of them is extraversion-introversion.

State of Mind (Attitude): Extraverted vs. Introverted Types

As a rule, all activity of extraverts is directed at an object and is determined by it. Extraverts see prime value in that object. Their life energy is almost entirely directed towards the object. Because of this, one of their strongest traits is, as Jung put it, «to be expended and expanded». These extravert characteristics define the unique energetic value of their psyche: they give off the impression of active, purposeful (sometimes expansive) people — their willful impulse is directed outward. In any case, the extraverted type has a tendency towards direct interaction with the outside world. Generally, they feel uninhibited in the choices of their surroundings; and due to this, they can easily change their surroundings to suit them. Most of the time, extraverts take the initiative in making acquaintances.

Introverts are concentrated mostly on their assessment of objects or events, not the object itself. The actions of introverts do not depend directly on outside influences; they are determined by their personal inner standing. Sometimes this is mistakenly judged as self-absorption and egotism. But it should never be forgotten that any perception and cognition is not only objective but subjective as well. The world exists not only as it is but as we perceive it to be.

Since introverts view the situation around them as a given, they do not attempt to change it, but rather try to adapt to it themselves. For example, they generally do not like taking the initiative in meeting new people. Instead, they wait until other people make their first move.

To summarize, one might say that extraverts want to take higher ground in order to better observe all the surrounding space and events happening there, while introverts perceive their «ego» as a protective shield behind which they are hiding, lurking out from time to time.

> **Extraverts** — *people focused on everything going on around them; are able to change a situation if it does not suit them; easily socialize both personally and professionally.*

> **Introverts** — *people focused on their inner feelings about one issue or another; adapt to situations instead of changing them; have difficulty making acquaintances in unfamiliar surroundings.*

It is possible to determine the «vertness» orientation as early as in the childhood years. Here are two characteristic examples where the difference between an introvert and an extravert can easily be distinguished.

> *My mother took me to the dance studio for the first time and, being in a hurry, left me in the locker room. While I was changing, the class started. That day I did not have the courage to enter the classroom on my own. Instead, I stood in front of the door for the entire lesson. I just was too shy to enter. Such things happened to me several times later.*

> *One of the liveliest recollections of my childhood was the exhibition concert in the first year of my music school. I was agitated, and still, I was sure that everything should be alright, so I was in a solemn and lofty mood, which quickly disappeared during the concert. I found that teachers did not indulge their students with variety of repertory, and all of them had to perform the same piece on their violins. Such a situation could make only parents of the young talents happy, while the rest of the audience watched the performance with unspeakable sadness.*

> *Did I expect such an attitude towards myself after spending an hour a day practicing my violin? Of course not! I do not remember exactly how I arrived at my subsequent actions, but everybody remembered my performance for a long time.*

I jumped onto the stage almost dancing and immediately started tortur-
ing my violin. At the same time I was singing a song about four little jolly
notes, not being too anxious about the listeners' eardrums. I decided that
it was not enough to just shock people, and the song was performed twice.
All this made my teacher panic, although I played much better the second
time. On the other hand, I enjoyed thunderous applause and greetings
from my mother and classmates, as well as the reaction of my teacher who
informed me later that she had never expected such a dirty trick from me.

Symbols of Jungian Functions

Now let us return to the first two dichotomies, thinking-feeling and sensation-intui-tion. Taking into account that each of these four poles may emerge in extraverted as well as introverted variants, we end up with eight Jungian functions. In Socionics, a certain symbol is assigned to each of the eight functions.

Table 1.2. **Symbols of Jungian functions**

	EXTRAVERTNESS	INTROVERTNESS
THINKING	■	☐
FEELING	◰	◳
SENSATION	●	○
INTUITION	▲	△

Thinking, feeling, sensation, intuition…To certain extent, each person possesses all of these four functions. However, extraverts, whose mind is focused directly on objects, must better actualize their extraverted functions («black functions» ■, ◰, ●, ▲.)

On the other hand, introverts, are focused on relations and their subjective attitude towards objects. They model various aspects of reality in their minds and better actual-ize their introverted functions («white functions»… ☐, ◳, ○, △.)

To summarize the meaning of the socionic functions, let us represent them in the following table.

Table 1.3. **Socionic Functions**

Symbol	Name	Manifestation of Functions
■	Practical Thinking	Business profit, efficiency, expediency, technology
□	Structural Thinking	Imaginative structure, scientific theories, systematization
▙	Emotional Feeling	Open emotional influence, immediate emotional reactions
▛	Relational Feeling	Human relationships, duty and morality, respect of traditions, guarding of principles
●	Volitional Sensation	Activeness, expansion, spatial control, assertiveness
○	Self-perceptive Sensation	Spatial harmony, contentedness, well-being
▲	Potentiality Intuition	Ability to assess the inner capacities and potential of the object
△	Temporal Intuition	Premonition, prediction, ability to perceive dynamics of development, poetics, mystic sense

Personality Program Determined by Each Jungian Function

It is not easy to formulate the basic personality program determined by each of the eight psychological functions. The problem is that the specific form of the program will be different for each individual depending on, their upbringing, culture, education, and many other factors. Therefore, each of the personality programs, described below has wide-rang of characteristics. Nevertheless, this program outlines the general principles that guide the consciousness of the individual belonging to a certain psychological type.

- ■ — Reality comes first. In order to survive, humans have to work efficiently, producing material profit. The only value of an idea is the possibility of its realization.

- □ — Everything in the world must comply with a certain order and system. This is the core of life on which everything else relies; if it is taken out, everything else collapses. It is crucial to understand this system, to develop and improve it, and to find everyone's place in it.

- ◣ — All actions are influenced by emotions such as happiness, anger, grief, depression, etc. Emotions dictate everything a person does. Due to this, controlling one's own emotions and those of the others is very important.

- ◳ — A normal life requires harmony in human relations. The most important thing is to determine the ideals of human life and human relationships. The norms of ethics and morals are crucial here. Actual relations with people must agree with these ideals.

- ● — Life is a constant battle, full of vigorous action. It is vital to train your will and tone your body in order to be ready for immediate response and prevail in a critical situation.

- ○ — The main condition for psychological equilibrium is balance, contentedness, and harmony in everything that constitutes a person's surroundings. For a normal life it is extremely important to have equally good physical health and perception of beauty, comfort, and content.

- ▲ — The most interesting thing in life is to find something new, and exciting, discover a fresh, appealing opportunity, meet an interesting new person, or conceive an unusual project. The world is full of mysteries and secrets that have yet to be uncovered.

- △ — The main value of the world is the infinite and abundant reign of personal imagination. This imagination will never grow boring because with its help new ideas, suggestions, and images appear so magically and easily. Imagination makes it possible to delve into the darkness of the past and the mist of the distant future, to grasp the world in its entirety, to capture the dynamics and tendencies of main events, and to predict the final result.

How does the behavior of each of these psychological types emerge in real life? Envision this hypothetical situation:

A small passenger bus is negotiating a barren road in a deeply forested narrow gorge with a stream down below. Suddenly, around the bend a moose dashes out of the woods in front of the bus. The driver slams on the brakes. The moose disappears silently into the forest, but the bus spins out of the road and crashes into a tree on the edge of a cliff. The windshield shatters, the engine dies, the driver appears to be wounded, but all of the passengers escape with only bruises and shocks. The bus is about to slide off of the cliff. The first passenger to recover is a man with a square, stubborn chin. He momentarily assesses the situation and quickly issues commands to open or smash the windows, get out of the bus, and stabilize the wheels as quickly as possible before the bus slides and falls. Naturally, this wielder of a square chin is a Volitional Senser ●.

Luckily, the driver is not badly injured. He is in shock from the crash, his wounds are bleeding, but his life is not in danger. He is helped out of the bus and is laid on someone's coat. One of the passengers, a somewhat plump, unhurried woman, gently tends to him. «Relax, relax, sonny, everything will be fine», she comforts the young driver as she dresses his wounds, strokes his head and hands, and pours tea out of a thermos that she happened to have in her travel bag. The mind of this caring woman with the gentle hands, who so quickly comforts the driver, is obviously directed by the Self-perception Sensing ○.

At the same time, a short, brawny passenger in a leather jacket is already fiddling with the engine, trying to figure out if it is possible to fix it, or if it is necessary to send someone for help. He reassures the driver that he has already found the problem and it may be possible to fix it on site. Most likely, dear reader, you have already recognized that this passenger is a Practical Thinker ■.

«But where is that young man in jeans, who entertained us with jokes for the whole trip?» worries a striking woman in a floor-length black coat and a purple hat. «Where has he disappeared to? Maybe he is injured and still on the bus!!!»

«I'm right here!» a voice comes from somewhere overhead. It turns out that the young man has already climbed the highest tree in order to survey their surroundings (Extraverted Intuiters ▲ are always interested in seeing as much new as possible) «Over there, about a mile away, there is a small village where someone could go to for help». He adds more ideas, each one more unexpected than the previous one. They are not taken seriously, however, since everyone has been calmed by the fact that the engine problem is not serious and they can fix it by themselves.

A tall, lean man in glasses, who had been pondering one of his ideas throughout the whole trip by taking notes in his small notebook and occasionally throwing a dark glance at the overly talkative passenger in the jeans, who was obviously disturbing his concentration, was now sketching a diagram of the road in his notebook, calculating the radius of the turn where the moose had so unexpectedly popped out. Addressing no one in particular, as if he is simply thinking aloud, the man declares, «It's a good thing that the driver slowed down to 30 miles per hour before the turn. At such an abrupt turn, if we had been driving at a higher speed, we all would have been down the cliff by now. It's fortunate that we're alive at all!» In this man we clearly recognize a Structural Thinker □.

The woman in the purple hat, who is overexcited by all that have happened, interrupts him. On the bus she had been intrigued by the silent passenger and now finds a perfect opportunity to strike up a conversation. «Yes, it's a nightmare; I still can't quite come to myself, and that horrible moose, where did it jump out from? You know,» she continues, «once, I was on a cruise in the Mediterranean, and can you imagine, right in front of our ship....». However, the man in glasses is too involved in his thoughts to make conversation. He stares into the distance beyond the lady, and feeling insulted, she pouts. She looks around for somebody who will want to listen to her story. She is directed by the Emotional Feeling ◤, and it is very difficult for her to calm down without pouring her feelings out to somebody. Glancing around, she finds a small group of passengers who have settled down on an old log underneath a tree.

An elderly man with gray hair and sorrowful eyes is telling a story of a good old moose to two boys and their grandmother. The 7 and 8 years old boys have never seen «such a beast» before, and they cannot calm down.

The woman in the purple hat, noticing that the elderly man has finished his story, approaches him. Suddenly, feeling emotionally tired and overwhelmed by the day's events, she spreads her hands, shakes her head, sinks onto the grass and declares, «No, I'll never survive this day».

The man compassionately bends down towards her and says, «You don't have to worry like this. Let's go over there. They're already starting a campfire. You relax, and everyone will get together soon. In time of difficulty, people always feel safer together. We'll feel better when we join the others». The lady is grateful to the elderly man. His mind is directed by the Relational Feeling ◳, and he tries to create psychological comfort.

Sitting apart from everyone else is a blond girl with dreamy blue eyes. She is gazing at the sky where stars have begun to appear. The girl's thoughts are far away from what is happening around her: «That's life. It is fast-burning, like twigs in a fire, and only the stars will remain here when we will be gone from this world...». Gradually, words form in her head and arrange themselves into poetry. Naturally, her mind is directed by the Temporal Intuition △.

Leading Block of a Psychological Type

Socionics uses two psyche models: the Model J, which contains four powerful Jungian functions, and the full Model A, in which all eight functions are included. The Model J is sufficient for the first acquaintance with socionics. According to Model J, the human psyche is the result of the combined actions of four «communication channels». We will number them in order of descending strength. Each of the functions occupies its «own» channel, not recurring in any others.

First, we will study the combined work of the first two strong functions, which we will call the «Leading Block of Psychological Type».

I. The first channel. This channel is the most influential one, and is called **the Personality Program Channel**, which to the great extent determines a person's psychological type. If the type is extraverted, the channel is occupied by an extraverted, «black» function. If it is introverted, it is occupied by an introverted, «white» function. People receive complete and objective information about the world through this channel. Their thoughts, actions, and often their profession depends one way or another on the type of a function operating in the Personality Program Channel. This is the same function that Jung described in his work *Psychological Types* as the most decisive for every person. If a person performs an action that contradicts their first channel, he or she worries about that action for a long time, seeing it as the least acceptable blunder it is possible to make—because the content of that first channel represents indisputable values for the individual:

■	— Why didn't I notice that the motor was rattling right away?
□	— I'm embarrassed that I couldn't solve such an easy problem!
▙	— I can't forgive myself for losing control and yelling!
∟	— How could I not notice her difficult emotional state?
●	— My weakness in that argument is unforgivable!
○	— How could I fail to look after my own son's health?
▲	— It was so stupid of me to miss an opportunity like that!
△	— It was just plain criminal not to see how this was going to turn out!

II. The second channel. This channel is called the Productive Channel. This is another dominant channel, the sphere of vigorous actions directed outward. The creative abilities of a person always correspond to the function residing in this channel. This is why in Socionics this channel is also called **Creative**. For example, an extraverted, «black» Feeling symbolizes a desire to share both happiness and grief with other people, to sympathize with people, and to inspire them; an introverted, «white» Sensation stimulates the creation of comfort and coziness; «white» Thinking initiates the creation of new theories; etc. If the first channel function determines the Personality Program of the psychological type, then the second channel function specifies **the Method of this Program Execution**.

Thus, we have defined the main mechanisms of action of the functions residing in the first and second channels, the two strong functions of Model J.

Now we can formulate the mindset for every psychological type, which is determined by the two stronger functions, residing in the Personality Program Channel and the Productive Channel. At the same time, for each of the psychological types, we will further designate an abbreviation as well as its characteristic name (for example, **ITI** — **I**ntuitive **T**hinking **I**ntrovert, the Critic).

All 16 mindsets, i.e. the 16 psychological types are described below.

The Occupational Mindsets

PRAGMATICS (Sensing + Thinking)
1. ■ ○, *Thinking-Sensing Extravert (TSE, The Professional)*
Factual reality is most important for TSEs. It is absolutely necessary for them to comprehend the properties of the material world's objects. (■ — personality program). The most sensible thing for Professionals is to contribute into this reality, acting thoroughly and carefully, maintaining high quality and organizing a comfortable workplace (○ — method of the program execution).

2. ○ ■, *Sensing-Thinking Introvert (STI, The Craftsman)*
Everything around Craftsmen must be aesthetic, comfortable, harmonious, proportional, and balanced (○ — personality program). The most certain path towards this goal is to deliver high-quality and dependable products (■ — method of the program execution).

3. ● □, *Sensing-Thinking Extravert (STE, The Organizer)*
STEs like the fact that the world is ruled by force, and they are ready to try their force against others for the sake of victory (● — personality program). For Organizers, only lucid, logical calculations will lead to the victory in any situation (□ — method of the program execution).

4. □ ●, *Thinking-Sensing Introvert (TSI, The Structurist)*
Life must be subjected to a certain system both in the material world and in the world of human relations (□ — personality program). If this system is disturbed, the willpower must be used to restore the order (● — method of the program execution).

RESEARCHERS (Intuition + Thinking)
5. ■ △, *Thinking-Intuitive Extravert (TIE, The Entrepreneur)*
TIEs' actions should always rely on factual reality (■ — personality program). For that purpose, it is important to learn how to manage, manipulate, and improve reality, and also how to make the best use of your time (△ — method of the program execution).

6. △ ■, *Intuitive-Thinking Introvert (ITI, The Critic)*

The ITIs' world is infinite, flowing, multi-faceted; its state is constantly changing. The purpose of individuals is to find their place in the never-ceasing flow of events (△ — personality program). For Critics, taking action makes sense only when the optimal time to apply their strength has been determined (■ — method of the program execution).

7. ▲ □, *Intuitive-Thinking Extravert (ITE, The Seeker)*

The ITEs' world is full of enigmas conveying unique opportunities (▲ — personality program). These enigmas can be unraveled and opportunities fully used if the fundamental underlying regularities are found (□ — method of the program execution).

8. □ ▲, *Thinking-Intuitive Introvert (TII, The Analyst)*

A certain set of laws underlies everything that happens around TIIs. These laws must be uncovered (□ — personality program). In order to do this, it is necessary to penetrate as deeply as possible into the real meaning of things, events, and processes (▲ — method of the program execution).

SOCIALISTS (Sensing + Feeling)

9. ◣ ○, *Feeling-Sensing Extravert (FSE, The Enthusiast)*

Emotions motivate FSEs in all of their actions. The greatest value is in positive emotions (◣ — personality program), which can be multiplied if Enthusiasts entertain the people around them by arranging things, creating comfort, and pleasing them with presents (○ — method of the program execution).

10. ○ ◣, *Sensing-Feeling Introvert (SFI, The Epicurean)*

The key aspect in SFIs' life is harmony, comfort, and the opportunity to experience pleasure (○ — personality program). The most delightful things in life are to invite friends over, to enjoy oneself and share with others the moments of happiness (◣ — method of the program execution).

11. ● ◰, *Sensing-Feeling Extravert (SFE, The Leader)*

All SFEs aspire for an expansion of their influence, are full of desire for power and fame (● — personality program). In order to reach these goals, they must learn how to control people by manipulating their weaknesses (◰ — method of the program execution).

12. ◰ ●, *Feeling-Sensing Introvert (FSI, The Guardian)*

For FSIs, the requirements of a normal life are harmony of human relations, observance of moral and ethical norms, and respect toward traditions (◰ — personality program). It is necessary to employ significant efforts for maintaining this system of values (● — method of the program execution).

HUMANISTS (Intuition + Feeling)
13. ■ △, *Feeling-Intuitive Extravert (FIE, the Performer)*
Life for FIEs is not complete without emotional strain and dramatic experiences (■ — personality program). The Performers just need to find the idea that captures the imagination of people and affects their emotions (△ — method of the program execution).

14. △ ■, *Intuitive-Feeling Introvert (IFI, The Romantic)*
For IFIs, the most important thing in the world is the blooming garden of their own imagination. With its help, it is possible to see into the past and future, to recognize the world in its entirety, capture the dynamics of events around them (△ — personality program), and then emotionally inspire people to desired activities (■ — method of the program execution).

15. ▲ ⌐, *Intuitive-Feeling Extravert (IFE, The Initiator)*
The most interesting and captivating thing in the IFEs' world is foreseeing the potential possibilities and directions of development in human society as well as in the field of technology and production (▲ — personality program), and organizing people towards execution of the recognized possibilities (⌐ — method of the program execution).

16. ⌐ ▲, *Feeling-Intuitive Introvert (FII, The Psychologist)*
The guidelines for FIIs' normal life are harmony of human relations, abiding by the norms of ethics and morals, and guarding of traditions (⌐ — personality program). Due to this, it is absolutely necessary for Psychologists to practice self-improvement, to train and exercise their inner spiritual life, and to look for real values in people (▲ — method of the program execution).

Now Table 1.1 can be presented in a more detailed version:

Table 1.4. **Socionic types by occupational mindsets**

SENSATION

I. PRAGMATICS:	**III. SOCIALISTS**:
■ ○ **Professional** (thinking-sensing extravert)	◣ ○ **Enthusiast** (feeling- sensing extravert)
○ ◼ **Craftsman** (sensing-thinking introvert)	○ ◣ **Epicurean** (sensing-feeling introvert)
● □ **Organizer** (sensing-thinking extravert)	● ◳ **Leader** (sensing-feeling extravert)
□ ● **Structurist** (thinking-sensing introvert)	◳ ● **Guardian** (feeling-sensing introvert)

THINKING ———————————————————— **FEELING**

II. RESEARCHERS:	**IV. HUMANISTS:**
◼ △ **Entrepreneur** (thinking-intuitive extravert)	◣ △ **Performer** (feeling-intuitive extravert**)**
△ ◼ **Critic** (intuitive-thinking introvert)	△ ◣ **Romantic** (intuitive-feeling introvert)
▲ □ **Seeker** (intuitive-thinking extravert)	▲ ◳ **Initiator** (intuitive-feeling extravert)
□ ▲ **Analyst** (thinking-intuitive introvert)	◳ ▲ **Psychologist** (feeling-intuitive introvert)

INTUITION

Jungian Model (Model J)

For each psychological type, the Jungian model includes four functions in such a way that they are arranged in the descending order of strength. We are already familiar with two strong functions residing in the first and the second channels, which constitute the leading block of a psychological type. The function residing in the first channel is energetically stronger than the one in the second. Now we can introduce the weaker channels. The functions, which occupy these channels are the alternatives to the first two functions; they are the weak poles of the corresponding dichotomies. For example, if Sensation is the strongest function in the first channel, then Intuition will reside in the fourth and the weakest channel. Also, if Thinking is the function in the second channel, then, accordingly, Feeling will be in the third channel.

The «vertness» (extra- or introversion) of the functions in the channels II, III, and IV is the same and always opposite to the «vertness» of the function in the first channel.

We will now examine the two weaker channels in more detail.

III. Third Channel. Here, there is a striving (often impossible to fulfill) to be in harmony with the world and yourself. A person reacts painfully to any kind of pressure applied through this channel. The psychological function residing in this channel becomes, as a result, vulnerable to outside intrusion. Because of this, the third channel is called — **Channel of the Least Resistance**, or **Vulnerable Channel**.

IV. Fourth Channel: This channel is usually called the **Suggestible Channel**. A person is most susceptible to outside influence through this channel. The psychological function residing in this channel is the weakest of the four. A person is not at all confident in matters dealing with this function and obviously requires outside correction. However, on the conscious level, the person is nearly oblivious to information in this field and hardly perceives it at all.

For example, let us consider Model J of the two psychological types: one intuitive — feeling extravert (the Initiator) and another one thinking — sensing introvert (the Structurist).

Table 1.5. **Two examples of model «J»**

Channel number	Intuitive-feeling extravert, the Initiator	Thinking-sensing introvert, the Structurist
I	▲	□
II	⌐	●
III	□	▲
IV	○	◤

It is easy to notice that these two types are quite different by their psychological strengths, and thus must be totally different in their manifestations. In fact, the first (IFE) is an extravert, the second (TSI) is an introvert, the first is a feeler while the second is a thinker, the first is an intuiter and the second is a senser.

From the positions of the psychical functions of these two types we can conclude the following:

1. *The intuitive-feeling extraverts* are spontaneous people who get to the roots of things by their «vision», who emotionally involve other people due to the Feeling function in their Second Channel.

2. *The thinking-sensing introverts* are people of the structure: they strive for it, follow it, and improve it. If somebody else is reluctant to follow this system, the TSIs act by volitional pressuring due to the Volitional Sensing in their Second Channel. It is obvious that IFEs' ingenious actions, and their inability to work systematically (Structural Thinking in the Third Channel) will extremely irritate TSIs. Now let us tell the reader a little secret: the famous composer Mozart was an IFE and his antagonist, Salieri, was a TSI, which explains some of the problems in their relationship. Here is what Salieri, the hero of M. Forman's movie «Amadeus», says about Mozart's music as he reads his notes:

> *It was inconceivable, impossible to believe! Without drafts, without a single correction! He covered paper with notes as if he heard them in his head! And the music– the music was perfect. Take one note away, and that will be a great loss. It was the Lord's own voice!*

Naturally, this approach to composition was impossible and even more, unrighteous, to Salieri himself, who wrote music strictly following the laws of harmony and who could not understand any other way of composing.

Here we need to make an important remark. The question of celebrities belonging to a specific psychological type always arises during lectures in Socionics and is discussed with interest. However, the reader should be warned that «distant identification» of celebrities should be considered as most probable hypothesis of the author — nothing more. To be sure of somebody's type, either personal acquaintance with the respective celebrity or a psychologically precise description of his or her personality by biographers is necessary. The more data about celebrities are available, the more precise determination of their psychological type is possible. Personal contact with celebrities is often difficult for obvious reasons. Biographers may distort psychological portraits of the people they describe. That is why various specialists in Socionics often disagree about socionic types of famous people. Moreover, socionic researchers often revise their conclusions and decide that a celebrity belongs to a different psychological type than they previously had thought if new additional information becomes available.

As for Mozart and Salieri, the author believes that the hypotheses regarding their psychological types are veritable enough due to a lot of information available about these composers.

Below, the Jungian Models of all 16 psychological types are presented.

Table 1.6. **The Jungian Models of all 16 psychological types**

Channel number	EXTRAVERTS							
I	■	■	▙	▙	●	●	▲	▲
II	○	△	○	△	□	⌐	□	⌐
III	△	○	△	○	⌐	□	⌐	□
IV	⌐	⌐	□	□	△	△	○	○
Type number	1	2	3	4	5	6	7	8

Channel number	INTROVERTS							
I	□	□	⌐	⌐	○	○	△	△
II	●	▲	●	▲	■	▙	■	▙
III	▲	●	▲	●	▙	■	▙	■
IV	▙	▙	■	■	▲	▲	●	●
Type number	9	10	11	12	13	14	15	16

Now we know the definitions of Jungian psychological functions, and therefore have mastered almost all basic notions necessary for the determination of psychological types. However, before using this main working tool of the new science, we need to make one more important step.

Rationality Vs. Irrationality

Look at Model J attentively. You will see that distribution of the functions residing in the channels for each of the 16 types is not arbitrary but strictly regular. Look at the functions in the pairs of channels I and IV, then II and III. Each of these pairs corresponds to a dichotomy, i.e. either Thinking-Feeling or Sensation-Intuition. Therefore, each of the two strongest channels, namely I and II, contains one pole of each of these dichotomies: e.g. one of them contains Thinking or Feeling, while the other contains Sensation or Intuition.

How does it happen? Is there any regular balance between the functions?

Now it is time to attribute one more important characteristic to each of the four psychological functions. We have already noticed certain dependency between opposites of each pair of psychological functions: strong Thinking implies weak Feeling and vice versa, and the same rule applies to Sensation and Intuition. First of all, this empirical fact is a proof of profound and organic relation between the poles of the dichotomies.

From all said above we can conclude that human consciousness that comprises the whole physical world can be split apart into two different fields of perception: thinking-feeling and sensing-intuitive (which corresponds to perception of matter-energy and space-time). Human psyche may be predominantly focused only on one of these two fields, which was established by Jung. Therefore, dominance of either thinking-feeling or sensing-intuitive perception constitutes one more alternative pair.

It is easy to understand that people with dominant Sensation (●, ○) or Intuition (▲, △) rely on their direct contact with the external world, while people with dominant Thinking (■, □) or Feeling (◣, ◰) lack such immediateness of perception. Thus the functions ■, □, ◣, ◰ represent specific, somewhat «distant» attitude towards objects of the outer world. Jung called types with dominant ■, □, ◣, ◰ Rational, and types with dominant ●, ○, ▲, △ — Irrational.

Therefore, Rationals are the types with dominant Thinking or Feeling, while Irrationals are those with dominant Sensation or Intuition. Rationals perceive the world indirectly, as if from certain psychological distance, which allows them to judge, to evaluate, to make decisions in advance, to set goals and plan actions, to control these actions by criteria of moral, ethics, sympathy-antipathy etc. They tend to do all their work consistently and to complete everything they start. If any circumstances intervene with the implementation of the Rationals' plans, they feel frustrated and uncomfortable. Sometimes it may happen that Rationals cannot switch to a different task, even though they really want to, as if a mysterious force prevents them from switching; they «get stuck» running in circles.

By contrast, irrational types are directly involved in events, they always «go with the flow», their actions depend not so much on their initial intentions as on circumstances. In their behavior, as seen by other people, they may be unpredictable and labile, and their lability directly depends on the constantly changing world around them. Irrational types can sometimes leave projects already started for the sake of new interesting ones.

In many other manifestations these two types of psyche act totally differently which we will demonstrate by the following examples:

— Rationals work according to a schedule, try to avoid risk, while Irrationals tend to make spontaneous decisions. Under influence of momentary impulse, Irrationals may take risks without thinking of consequences;

— Uncertainty and ambiguity make life difficult for Rationals because they cannot predict and plan under such circumstances, while for Irrationals the state of ambiguity is their natural domain, and «overly organized» life is boring and depressing;

— These two types react differently to the jet lag after long flights: Irrationals adapt much easier while Rationals take it harder.

Let us consider the following example:

> *Here is how our day begins: I wake up always at the same time, do my morning exercises, and then spend some time reading, knitting or studying. Then I get tired and hungry and start cooking breakfast. At this moment my roommate wakes up, but it takes some time for her to get out of bed. When breakfast is ready, I have to hurry her up. As a result, I sit alone at the table and wait for her so that we can have breakfast together. Sometimes, her friend comes to stay with us. The two of them can snore half the day away, get hungry at midnight and start frying potatoes.*

In this case the storyteller certainly is a Rational while her roommate and her friend are Irrationals.

Now we have all necessary tools to describe characteristic psychological traits of representatives of each of the 16 types based on Model J. This requires describing their psyche by all the four dichotomies. As a reminder, here is a short description of each of the two poles of the four dichotomies:

Extraverts — focused on everything that happens around them, can change situations which they do not like, easily start new personal or business contacts.

Introverts — focused on their internal attitudes towards certain events, prefer to adapt to the situation rather than changing it, have difficulties in establishing contacts with unfamiliar people.

Rationals — prefer planning their activities in advance, hardly switch from one activity to another, generally avoid multitasking, strive for completion and closure of ongoing projects.

Irrationals — guided by the power of their perception, easily switch to a different task and can perform several tasks simultaneously, can be distracted from the projects they have started.

Thinkers — focused on objective reality, physical laws of the world, production processes; such people hold their ground, value professionalism.

Feelers — are emotional personalities although they do not necessarily manifest their emotions externally. Feelers depend on opinions of the others, easily get involved in emotional conflicts, can choose correct psychological distance while communicating with other people.

Sensers — perceive the world in specific details, live in the «here and now», value comfort and know how to provide it, enjoy practical activity, and prefer clear material outcomes of their work.

Intuiters — perceive the world as a whole, tend to daydream, experiment, and generate many ideas which might not be easy to implement. They can be absent-minded, value perspectives over material gains.

Part II
PSYCHOLOGICAL TYPES

The complete table of psychological types is presented below. The most commonly used designations of the psychological types (both socionic terms and characteristic names) are given in the right column.

The symbols of the functions for each psychological type are represented strictly by the positions of the channels from left to right (first to fourth.) This means that the function that is farthest to the left resides in the Personality Program channel; the next function is located in the Productive channel, and so on.

The abbreviations in the table are as follows: I (in the beginning) — Intuitive; I (in the end) — Introvert; T — Thinking; S — Sensing; F — Feeling; E — Extravert. For example: IFI — Intuitive Feeling Introvert.

Think over the information presented in the table. At first glance, there arises a multitude of questions. For example, why are there only 16 psychological types? There must be many more combinations than that! Why are the functions arranged exactly in that way, and not another way? Why does only one channel dominate a person's psyche, and not two or three? Can only eight functions be used to identify a person's psychological type?

Not all these questions have a logical answer. When the matter concerns the human psyche, all rules are established on the basis of lengthy observations, as well as clinical practices. The observations started by Carl Gustav Jung determined that only one function out of eight, which resides in the first channel, dominates in the human psyche. This function must first of all agree with the «vertness» (i.e., extra- or introversion) of the individual. In addition, it must have precise orientation on the «rationality-irrationality» axis and then, in this area, thinking-feeling, or sensing-intuitive traits have to be determined.

Table 2.1
Socionic Types and their Model J.

Jungian criteria				Model J Channels				Types
				I	II	III	IV	
INTROVERT	Labile	Feelers	Intuit	△	◣	■	●	Intuitive-Feeling Introvert (IFI, Romantic)
			Sens.	○	◣	■	▲	Sensing-Feeling Introvert (SFI, Epicurean)
		Thinkers	Intuit	△	■	◣	●	Intuitive-Thinking Introvert (ITI, Critic)
			Sens..	○	■	◣	▲	Sensing-Thinking Introvert (STI, Craftsman)
	Rationality	Feelers	Intuit	⌐	▲	●	■	Feeling-Intuitive Introvert (EFI, Psychologist)
			Sens.	⌐	●	▲	■	Feeling-Sensing Introvert (FSI, Guardian)
		Thinkers	Intuit	□	▲	●	◣	Thinking-Intuitive Introvert (TII, Analyst)
			Sens.	□	●	▲	◣	Thinking-Sensing Introvert (TSI, Structurist)

Jungian criteria				Model J Channels				Types
				I	II	III	IV	
EXTRAVERT	Labile	Feelers	Intuit	▲	⌐	□	○	Intuitive-Feeling Extravert (IFE, Initiator)
			Sens.	●	⌐	□	△	Sensing-Feeling Extravert (SFE, Leader)
		Thinkers	Intuit	▲	□	⌐	○	Intuitive-Thinking Extravert (ITE, Seeker)
			Sens.	●	□	⌐	△	Sensing-Thinking Extravert (STE, Organizer)
	Rationality	Feelers	Intuit	◣	△	○	□	Feeling-Intuitive Extravert (FIE, Performer)
			Sens.	◣	○	△	□	Feeling-Sensing Extravert (FSE, Enthusiast)
		Thinkers	Intuit	■	△	○	⌐	Thinking-Intuitive Extravert (TIE, Enterpreneur)
			Sens.	■	○	△	⌐	Thinking-Sensing Extravert (TSE, Professional)

41

The function that resides in the second, Productive Channel must possess at least two essential qualities:

1. It is «vertness» should be the opposite of the first function. If the function (the one residing in the first channel) is introverted, then the second one must be extraverted and vice-versa.

2. The function operating in the second channel must be on the other pole of rationality-irrationality axis in relation to the first one. That is, if the first channel is occupied by a rational function, then the function in the second channel must be irrational and vice versa.

These two requirements for the second channel can be substantiated very easily: the psyche of any normal person must be in a state of balance. Due to this, the two strongest functions must complement and compensate each other.

Therefore, our psyche is inherently asymmetrical, and any person, if isolated from society, cannot adequately perceive the world in its entirety. This inadequacy is different for each of the 16 psychological types. So the representatives of all 16 types with their own psychological advantages can be helpful to the others in their own unique ways. This leads all of us to recognize the necessity of integration with people of other psychological types in order to compensate for this asymmetry. The minimal level of such compensation is achieved by bringing together a pair of individuals whose functions are reversed. In Socionics, this kind of pairing is known as dual pairing.

The next step of integration is the Quadra, a group of four people positioned so that in each row, all four functions are present (two «white» and two «black») — we will consider the Quadras in Part III addressing intertype relationships. Theoretically, the ideal integration includes all 16 socionic psychological types. Such a group is capable of perceiving and reflecting the surrounding world in its entirety. It is assumed that each of the types belongs to the same cultural background and the «strong» functions of the individuals are equally developed.

There is one more consideration which we shall discuss before proceeding to the description of the psychological types.

Our research indicates that two functions of the leading block of the same type can be represented differently, namely, one of them may be enhanced. Let us recall that introverts have an introverted function in the first channel of the leading block, and the function in the second channel is extraverted. Assume that the first function is substantially enhanced. In this case individuals are deeply immersed in themselves, are constantly preoccupied with their thoughts, and barely react to the outside world.

What if another representative of the same psychological type has an enhanced function in the second channel? How will it manifest itself? Since this function is extraverted, this individual will be rather communicative, open, and social; his or her reactions will clearly reveal the qualities of an extravert.

Analogous considerations may also be applied to extraverts: they can either be strongly extraverted (if the function in the first channel is enhanced) or reveal some introverted qualities (if the function in the second channel is enhanced).

Similarly, rational types with enhanced function in the first channel will be very rigid in manifestations of their rationality, while those with enhanced function in the second channel (which is irrational for the rational types) will be more flexible.

The reader might ask: is it possible that enhancement of a certain function in the leading block lead to conversion to a different type? For instance, would not a TSE (the Professional) ■ ○ with enhanced Sensation be identical to a STI (the Craftsman) ○ ■ with enhanced Thinking? Socionic research proves that it is not so. In this example a TSE remains extraverted and rational, though these qualities are somewhat weakened by the enhanced function in the second channel. Moreover, as we have discussed, the roles of the first and the second channels are principally different.

In Socionics, the enhancement of one of the strong functions is indicated in the characteristic name of the psychological type. For example, if a «sensing Craftsman» is discussed, it means that a specific representative of STI type has enhanced Sensation, while a «thinking Craftsman» has enhanced function (Thinking) in the second channel. As a result, each of the 16 psychological types can be divided into two subtypes.

TEMPORAL INTUITION: ROMANTIC AND CRITIC

The Model J of these two types uses the following functions:

△ — **Temporal Intuition.** Presentiment, prediction, perception of dynamics in development, poetical spirit, mysticism (I, Personality Program, for the both types).

◣ — **Emotional Feeling.** Susceptibility to emotions, direct emotional influence, exposed feelings (II, Productive, for the Romantic and III, Vulnerable, for the Critic).

◼ — **Practical Thinking.** Pragmatism, efficiency, rationality, affection to technology (II, Productive, for the Critic and III, Vulnerable, for the Romantic).

● — **Volitional Sensing.** Persuasive pressure, determination, persistence, spatial control (IV, Suggestible, for the both types).

THE ROMANTIC: Intuitive-Feeling Introvert (I F I)
△, ◣, ◼, ●

General appearance

Type ROMANTIC

Natural grace is the most prominent feature of Romantics (IFIs) that sets them apart from other psychological types. This trait can show itself in refined clothing or elegant movements, regardless of physique.

Among strangers, Romantics are very mistrustful, fretting and worrying. They are reluctant to talk about themselves or their friends with outsiders. A bashful smile appears on their faces, as if asking everyone to forgive them. Their behavior is very gentle and polite, revealing tact and politeness. However, in a group of close friends or with family they can act fussy and sometimes even rude.

Characterization According to Strong Channel Functions

I. Personality Program Channel (△ — presentiment, prediction...)

A Romantic feels like being carried by a powerful stream of time, which is impossible and inexpedient to overcome.

> *This guy has a characteristic trait. He is a good indicator of other people's possibilities and perspectives. He is like a weathercock pointing to those who are about to be successful. His attitude to you is a faultless signal whether you are OK or you are losing tempo.*

Romantics often daydream. The subject of these daydreams can be a change of career, a perfect love, or going on an adventure. Many books about the paranormal (occultism, bioenergetics, alternative medicines) can often be found in their homes.

For Romantics time has substance. Dreamers and poets, Romantics easily disconnect from reality and wander in the land of imagination where they find the joy and meaning of life. Living through an adventure in this imaginative land for them is the same as to accomplish something practical for the others.

They often muse about themselves and their abilities, and strive to understand themselves. Sometimes, the representations of this psychological type seek extra-sensory abilities within themselves. They analyze their abilities of influencing people. It's hard to imagine these people without belief in anything; it's essential for them to have some kind of ideal. With the downfall of one model, they search for another.

They are gullible and impressionable. If they are told it will bring good luck, they will knock on wood or carry a good luck charm.

They often hesitate in making decisions.

Romantics sense imminent danger very well, and either try to prevent it or warn those around them.

Emotionally negative experiences leave a deep mark on his mind, but positive feelings leave behind only the tiniest trace. When showing someone her wedding photo, a Romantic woman said,

> *I look like someone who is about to give away her freedom.*

II. Productive channel (▙ — emotionality...)

Romantics don't hide their feelings, and can sometimes burst out laughing, start crying, or get angry at someone in public. In front of family or close friends, they can even be outright rude. Romantics love to tell people about their problems. Here, one woman relates an incident involving her acquaintance, who is a Romantic:

> *Yesterday I met a friend. She was very upset and said she was divorcing her husband. «What? Why?» I asked. «Because he hasn't brought me flowers for more than a week! Does your husband give you flowers?» «No.» I said: «He hasn't bought me any gifts for a long time.*

Well, I don't understand how you can live with a man who doesn't bring you flowers!

Romantics love to be the center of attention: they readily organize parties for nearly every possible occasion, though it saps their strength. They think up an imaginative program for every party, plan fun group games, make craft, create exquisite dishes, and give an aesthetic touch to everything. Romantics are capable of being very sweet, effortlessly socializing with large groups, and complimenting people in order to leave a good impression (○). They enjoy art, love music and poetry, and like to decorate their house with their own handwork (○).

Romantics sense even the weakest emotions of others. They strives to lend a hand, to console those facing hardships, to find the right words to cheer someone up.

Characterization According to Weak Channel Functions

III. Vulnerable Channel (■ — pragmatism, efficacy)

It's difficult for Romantics to work hard at anything business-related. For example, they plan to take courses at a community college, but after the first few classes, they can't take the pressure and drop out. This is how most of their attempts at fulfilling business responsibilities, duties, or chores turn out.

Romantics work well under a volitional manager who sets tasks in the way of «fulfill or lose your job». When the manager is liberal, a Romantic begins to hesitate; working turns into long discussions without any outcome.

It is usually hard for Romantics to keep their house always tidy. While washing the dishes, they can stop halfway through for a snack, not continuing afterwards. It's also hard for them to keep their finances in order. Money can be left lying around the house. Romantics buy things spontaneously, often spending money on appealing, yet unnecessary, purchases. As a result, their house is full of useless things: gaudy umbrella stands, fancy vases, books they will never read, various antique statues, lacy tablecloths, and so on.

IV. Suggestible channel (● — determination, persistence, drive…)

Romantics are followers, not leaders. It's difficult for Romantics to use willpower, they would prefer that somebody guides them in the right direction, infect them with energy, or, best of all, do the task for them. As a rule, Romantics easily locate such people around them and, using their abilities as Feelers, persuade them to do what is necessary by demonstrating fragility, evoking sympathy (even pity), etc. Romantics can easily find others' weaknesses, and use them to get what they want.

The best way to use a Romantics' business capabilities is to set clear boundaries for accomplishing a task that, if at all possible, requires creativity.

Job Options

The best job for IFIs is one that doesn't concern academics. Some examples of good job choices are musicians, authors, tour guides, journalists, talk show hosts, etc. Sometimes IFIs can be found doing well in the field of mathematics. However, keep in mind that the worst jobs for this psychological type concern business and administration.

Famous IFIs: composer — Frederic Chopin, writers — Hans Christian Andersen, Ray Bradbury, politicians — Nikolai Bukharin (Russian revolutionary), Yuri Gagarin (the first man to fly to the space).

THE CRITIC:
Intuitive-Thinking Introvert (ITI)
△, ■, ◤, ●

General Appearance

Type CRITIC

Critics' (ITIs) frowns and sullen expressions distinguish them from others. An onlooker might think that the Critic is criticizing them.

The figure is most often heavyset and bulky. Those who have strong intuitive functions may appear unkempt. They don't pay attention to their appearance, causing those around them to want to look after them. In socializing, they are often gentle, courteous, and tactful. However, those with strong logic functions are neat and orderly. Critics can be aggressive when their interests are threatened.

Characterization According to Strong Channel Functions

I. Personality Program Channel (△ — premonition, prediction...)

Critics perceives, the world in its entirety and themselves as part of this completeness. They are philosophers, constantly watching the never-ending stream of events around them. For Critics, life is like a river, sometimes calm, at other times turbulent, with the surface shifting and changing with every moment. This is why it can be hard for them to make decisions, they strive to consider all possibilities under changing circumstances. For Critics, one of the most important things in life is being within this stream of events, surging with it, but at the same time they must choose their «personal stream», the one that's flowing in the right direction. Sometimes it happens like this:

> *My friend and I traveled from Arkansas to Niagara Falls for free, by hitchhiking. We stood by the side of the road until a car or a truck came by, and then we'd ask the driver how far he could take us. When he dropped us off as near to our destination as he could, we waited for another car, and started the whole thing over again. We plan to return the same way.*

Critics are good at sensing a possible turn of events, and can foretell them. However, these predictions are usually pessimistic. A Critic often anticipates a change for the worse or the arrival of hard times. At times, they feel that they know everything in advance, and life holds no surprises for them. This can sometimes cause the Critic to fall into a melancholy. Every new acquaintance seems like an old friend, and this friend's actions are easily guessed. Their predictions about new acquaintances can indeed be very accurate, especially if they have had the chance to socialize with the person for a while. This causes people to consider Critics very wise and far-seeing.

The constant focus on foreseeing and the necessity of considering every tiny detail in any undertaking causes uncertainty and doubts for Critics.

Critics tend to scrutinize even the simplest question. They dislike sharp changes, preferring a gradual path to progress, and they move towards their goals slowly but surely.

II. Productive Channel (■ — pragmatism, efficiency...)

Since Critics is able to look from above at all the complex events, they endeavors to direct this action to a practical purpose. Once they correctly predict the final result, they can sit back and wait for a convenient moment to carry out their plan. Critics will never perform a useless task, but, if they feel that there is a real benefit, they act immediately. They are secretive and cautious in business relations. Critics don't pay much attention to their promises and may put them aside for some time. A fear of overlooking details causes them to be very careful when making decisions: when in an administrative post, they may delay signing business papers for a long time.

The work capabilities of Critics are very selective. If they find the job that's right for them, they may show wild energy and fantastic work capacity.

If they don't find the right job, their skepticism overwhelms everything else, and they become too lethargic to perform even the most basic tasks of life.

> *During the whole business day he is not an architect of his own time; he is like a boat without oars, in the grip of other people and circumstances. However, when the working day ends and everybody goes home, he can calmly do his main job — strategic issues in development of our enterprise.*

Characterization According to Weak Channel Functions

III. Vulnerable Channel (⬕ — emotionality...)

Critics consider excessive emotions to be detrimental, as they interfere with level-headed analysis of any situation.

> *I thought I was quite incapable of having strong feelings, and only later I realized that love may be of different kinds. Feelings never fill me totally; on the contrary, reasonable balance between the sensual, emotional and rational love makes me constant in my attachment to my girlfriend, who I have been with for several years.*

As Critics don't sense the emotional mind-set of others, they can be quite tactless in dealing with people who come to them for sympathy — instead of consoling, they can attempt to «reason» about what happened and explain that it was only to be expected. In their social life, Critics may assign people roles which they are not accustomed to. In this «assigning», they fully believe in their scenario and expect it to be true. When their predictions don't match reality, they search for a reason and continue to consider themselves as all-knowing. Critics really love teaching and disciplining, not always understanding whether it is good or bad in the current situation. At the same time, their weakness in the emotional channel often results in that they cannot deny help to those who ask for it, and may spend the entire workday helping others, leaving their own business to fall by the wayside.

IV. Suggestible channel (● — determination, persistence, drive...)

Among Critics, totally opposite personal willpowers can be found. Some of them are extremely persistent and single-minded, others have no willpower whatsoever. This situation also applies to one Critic: in some matters he/she is relentless, in others completely lazy.

They listen to close friends and family in personal matters:

> *During the summer, we went hiking in the wilderness. Every evening, he (a Critic) would set out to the nearest town to send his mother a telegram, telling her he was alive and well. He did this with no protest at all, because she had asked him to.*

Job Options

The abilities of a ITI are utilized wherever a strategic prognosis is needed, which can be in politics, finance, or the military. ITIs can also successfully apply themselves in the field of science. Often, they become the sagacious directors of entire institutes, determining the most advantageous direction of the development of each laboratory. Industrial sciences, natural sciences, philosophy, and art may interest them as well.

Famous ITIs: actors Giulietta Mazina, Sergey Bondarchuk, scientists — Carl Gustav Jung, Isaac Newton, philosopher — Socrates; writers — Honore de Balzac, Leo Tolstoy, Joseph Brodsky, Gabriel Garcia Marquez, Thomas Mann, composers — Richard Wagner, Ludwig van Beethoven politicians —Charles de Gaulle, Wincton Churchill.

SELF-PERCEPTIVE SENSING: EPICUREAN AND CRAFTSMAN

The Model J of these two types uses the following functions:

○ — **Self-perceptive.** Sensing, spatial harmony, contentedness, well-being (I, Personality Program, for the both types).

◣ — **Emotional Feeling.** Emotionality, open emotional influence, immediate emotional reaction (II, Productive, for the Epicurean and III, Vulnerable, for the Craftsman).

■ — **Practical Thinking.** Pragmatism, efficacy, expediency, technology (II, Productive, for the Craftsman and III, Vulnerable, for the Epicurean).

▲ — **Potentiality Intuition.** Ability to assess inner capacity and potential of a phenomenon (IV, Suggestible, for the both types).

THE EPICUREAN: Sensing-Feeling Introvert (SFI)
○, ◣, ■, ▲

General Appearance

The face and silhouette are soft and round-shaped. The figure lacks a distinct waist and is often plump. The imaginative taste of the Epicureans (SFI) shows up in refined, even stylish, attire. Epicureans are very friendly in their interactions with others. They are informal, easygoing, but not inopportunate. The amount of independence in their lifestyle may be surprising. They enjoy casual conversation, with their own colorful details added.

Type EPICUREAN

Characterization According
to Strong Channel Functions

I. Personality Program Channel (○ — harmony, comfort, well-being...)

Epicureans' major credo is that humans were made to be happy and enjoy life — not some day, but every day. Hence, they need comfort and easy living conditions in order to be happy. A messy workplace makes it impossible for Epicureans to concentrate. So, they begin a work day by cleaning up their study, preparing a comfortable light level, and, relieved and contented, finally doing their job with great delight. The same applies to cooking, washing, and other housekeeping chores: everything around them has to be neat, so as not to get on their nerves. Defective tools, such as a leaky pen, or an overly blunt pencil are yet another source of distress. If there is no choice but to live with a mess, they feel lethargic, discouraged and consider themselves failures.

Epicureans revive memories of their past by the feelings they experienced at those moments:

> *I remember myself a toddler climbing a playpen with my friend. I fell down and hurt my head. I remember this pain very well, and what followed it: I sat on the floor, feeling pain mixed with distress. I was mad that I couldn't do things as well as my friend. When I started crying, my mom rushed to comfort me from the kitchen and gave me a hug — I remember that very vividly. I recall my friend's heels right under my nose, the rails of the playpen, huge Lego blocks — they don't seem so big now.*

It may be that while walking in the street, an Epicurean is struck with a strong scent of, say, a man's cologne. If this is a familiar scent — a friend's cologne, even if the friend used it only once, then Epicureans are caught by the feelings tied to the friend: attraction, antipathy, boredom, or embarrassment. Sometimes these feelings are so overwhelming that Epicureans may find themselves talking with this person in their mind.

Epicureans' perfect artistic taste helps them to choose nice clothing, find cosmetics to wear, and so on, all by themselves.

II. Productive Channel (■ — emotionality...)

Epicureans are skillful in recognizing human emotions and managing them. They don't usually argue and rarely get mad: if the disputed issue is not important, they back away. If they feel their words may hurt someone's feelings, they will turn them into a joke. Epicureans try to escape scandals at any cost. A quarrel in the family is a real tragedy for them. To avoid this, they try to talk to everybody individually, carefully and seriously consider each person's behavior, try to comfort each member of the family and divert them from the argument, and, in the end, convince everybody of the benefit of peace. If they do not accomplish their goal promptly, they would find another way to do it, with less effort and tension.

> *For a long time I have dreamt about having a cat, but my parents were against it saying that our guinea pig was enough. Once, when*

I visited my aunt, I saw him — a small fluffy ball with huge eyes, all black with three white spots. I decided at once that he would be mine.

When my dad opened the door to let me in, he didn't notice anything because I hid the cat in a bag. I let him go in the kitchen, and he meowed pitifully. My Dad got furious and demanded that I get rid of him by tomorrow! I talked him into leaving the cat until the next weekend, promising to bring him back to my aunt then. Next Sunday I said that my aunt was expecting guests and it was not the right day to return the cat. By that time, my mom had gotten used to the new family member, and I kept looking for reasons to get his return postponed. A month passed, and the kitten, who is still with us, found its way into even my father's heart.

Epicureans are attracted to love in all its many forms. A teenaged Epicurean would fall in love to see «what kind of passion he/she has for me», rather than have a real crush. If no passion is noticeable, the Epicurean seeks another admirer. In family life, Epicureans are also concerned with keeping feelings alive and would take prompt steps to achieve this goal (i.e. parting for a while) if needed.

Epicureans are not tolerant of betrayal and deception:

We all admired our boss. When he turned out to be a dishonest man, we were very disappointed. We all left, taking with us our memories of good times that we had together. After some time many of us returned to the club. As for me, I was not able to come back in spite of my longing for my old friends, as if some invisible barrier separated us: I cannot stand our boss any more.

Epicureans try not to compel anybody and restrain from punishing anybody, including their own children. If a reprimand takes place, five minutes later they feel deeply repentant.

Epicurean-supervisors strive to create a welcoming emotional climate in their team and to avoid contact with unpleasant people in business relations. They also care about employees' contentment. In return, Epicureans expect diligence and discipline from them.

Characterization According to Weak Channel Functions

III. Vulnerable Channel (■ — pragmatism, efficacy...)

«Pragmatic logic» is an underdeveloped and fragile function of Epicureans. Its weakness is revealed in the inability to act in a logical, rational way with minimal time and less effort.

Epicureans have a problem with boring, tedious jobs. Doing their best to avoid it, they try to work on something more appealing and enjoyable instead. A promise given by Epicureans may be forgotten and not fulfilled if they get distracted by some fascinating temptation. Afterwards, the Epicurean feels upset and is reluctant to meet the person he or she let down.

A real fans of pleasures, Epicureans are reluctant to demand unpleasant work from others. Epicureans feel hurt if someone points out their inability to work rationally. They are not interested in social standing, preferring the simple delights of everyday life and genial relations with friends.

While establishing business contacts, Epicureans would often take advantage of their personal connections. Epicureans are not skilled at working at a timely manner and therefore prefer to share responsibilities with others. When organizing social events, Epicureans would enjoy a secondary advisory role, suggesting somebody more capable than themselves for the main administrative function.

IV. Suggestible Channel (▲ — potential abilities, conceptual alternatives, generalizations...)

Epicureans are not always perfect in assessing the situation and acting accordingly. A woman of this type says:

> *I used to live by the carpe diem principle. I do not like to make plans for the future: it seems to me that when I plan anything in advance, there will necessarily be something that throws a wrench into them.*

They may misevaluate people by overestimating their positive traits. Always in good spirits and ready for pleasures, they live in the present day as if their future is free of problems. It would be wrong to assume, however, that they are not concerned at all about future. Anxiety about future is reflected in the way they prepare their children for life's hardships. Many Epicureans consider that a good education and a reliable occupation are the best guarantees for a safe, happy life. Epicureans are not good at evaluating the possible outcome of any endeavor and therefore rely on different sources of information. They are grateful to anybody who can offer suggestions on this matter.

Job Options

The best jobs for SFIs are in the field of human services. They make outstanding performers, musicians, painters, and can also work successfully in medicine or teaching. SFIs abilities can be best utilized in the areas of architecture, interior decorating, fashion design, or productive cooking.

Famous SFIs: actors — Marcello Mastroianni, Danny De Vito, Silvia Kristel, musician — Paul McCartney, writers — Alexander Dumas (the father), Andre Maurois.

THE CRAFTSMAN:
Sensing-Thinking Introvert (STI)
◯, ■, ◣, ▲
General Appearance

Appearance of a typical Craftsman (STI) is remarkable for its solidity, especially the Thinking subtype: these are strongly-built people who stand fast on their feet (like Inspector Maigret in Georges Simenon's novels). In general, people of the Thinking subtype of this type have more corpulent constitution than those of the Sensing subtype. Craftsmen prefer sporty or elegant styles in their dressing. Men of this type usually have somewhat loose and sprightly tread.

In communication they keep a distance up to the point of seeming cold, preferring not to demonstrate their emotions. Their comments are usually skeptical, and they uphold their standpoint very persistently.

Type CRAFTSMAN

Characterization According
to Strong Channel Functions

I. Personality Program Channel (◯ — harmony, comfort, health...)

The most important things for Craftsmen are their feelings of beauty, harmony, comfort and the sense of well-being. Everything should be balanced, harmonious and at the same time, expedient: in work, relations with others, choice of home furniture, and physically sound development of the body. Craftsmen associate the feelings of beauty and harmony with expediency (II — ■). They care for convenient working conditions, whether in a scientific lab or on their backyard.

Very often people of this type like to travel, maybe because traveling gives them a good opportunity to apply their sensing capabilities.

> *It is hard to describe how I like swimming in a sea in the middle of a storm. It charges me for a week with positive emotions; it gives me the feelings of harmony and relaxation in my body. When I feel discomfort, I go swimming...*

Another time the same person said:

> *Well, if I had such opportunity, I would spend all my vacations on tourist trips.*

However, a Craftsman never forgets about expediency even during vacations.

> *I like traveling to Crimea. There, I organized a diving club for children and I spend a lot of time with them. For this reason, I quite forgot about traveling to the ocean; there is nothing to do but swim.*

They are very sensitive to touches and do not allow those they do not like to touch them. Craftsmen do not like excessive volitional pressure, even for the sake of order:

> *It is hard for me to watch a child cry as his parents pull him to the kindergarten.*

Craftsmen have excellent memory for sensing details, and can stereoscopically recollect a picture from a certain period of their life, up to the smell of a roast rabbit in wine eaten decades ago.

II. Productive Channel (■ — Pragmatism, Efficacy...)

Craftsmen are usually perfect specialists in their narrow field. They do their work perfectly, using all possible options for optimization. For example, as hand workers, they know all the characteristics of materials, their products are not only useful but also esthetically pleasing.

They work calmly and methodically, but need that the final result to be expedient — they will scarcely make something of dubious usefulness. When they are certain about the expediency, they accomplishe their work with persistency. When a Craftsman's boss annoys her with numerous illogical and/or contradictory errands, she avoids arguments but rather attempts to calmly wind them down.

> *I am never content with phrases like «It is possible that...» I always need to know how precisely I will get the result. I rarely trust data given by other people — instead, I prefer to verify everything on my own experience, to check all possible options.*

If a Craftsman finds anybody of his colleagues unpleasant, he tries to organize the work in such a way that contact with the annoying person is decreased to a minimum. Otherwise, arguments will impede work. When he feels that the order is beyond his real possibilities, he easily recognizes this fact before a boss.

Characterization According to Weak Channel Functions

III. Vulnerable Channel (⬛ – emotionality...)

They seem moderate and passionless, preferring to hide their emotions. However, their reaction to insults, especially in public, may be explosive:

> *When I was a freshman in high school, there was a group of children of very important parents in our class. Some of the kids at school bent to this group, others even sought their protection. I held aloof from them, but they terrorized everybody and, one day, one of them hit me. I hit the offender in return. Other kids held us apart, but we agreed to fight after classes. I won the fight and won their respect, but even after that I never wanted to join this group of villains.*

Craftsmen are afraid that their feelings may be ridiculed, and for this reason are very secretive, in spite of their susceptibility. Sometimes, people of this type like spending time with children, because «it is easy to be natural with them».

Craftsmen feel hurt when their family members are indifferent to their emotional state and mood, and cannot just ignore, like some other types, unjust reproaches, especially because they hate to explain themselves.

> *I worked in my vegetable garden up to night under rain, had not a dry thread on, was as tired and hungry as a hunter and my wife complains about my late coming!*

They remember such offences for a long time, even though they do not express them verbally.

IV. Suggestible Channel (▲ – potential possibilities, alternatives, intellectual creativity ...)

It is not easy for Craftsmen to decide on a new undertaking – they will rather prefer to test everything before starting any activity, to make «little practical tests» whose outcomes will allow them to make judgments on whether the new enterprise is really necessary, and whether gains will overweigh expenses.

Sometimes it happens that they doubt their real capabilities and talents. Craftsmen hate the leveling approach, because in this case they lose bearings and cannot determine which positive capabilities and talents distinguish them from other people. For this reason, a Craftsman is attracted to people who understand talent, value it and can stimulate it.

Job Options

The best field of application of STIs inborn capabilities is any practical activity where they can work more or less independently or in a small group, where they will be valued as professionals and will not have to coordinate their activities with a lot of other people whose interests may be contradicting or conflicting. They do not strive for being Big Bosses; when STIs become managers or leaders, they manage the group calmly, without perusal of their authority.

A good sense of physical state and comfort (both their own and of other people) often allows STI to apply their talents in medicine or in sports (most often in individual sports, like skiing or swimming).

Actors of this type, being emotionally weak, compensate it with realism in their roles, and with over-attention to smallest details. Musicians of this type are often known for their perfect technique in performance.

Famous STIs: actors — Jean Gabin, Oleg Basilashvili, writers — William Somerset Maugham, Agatha Christie, Georges Simenon, Francoise Sagan.

RELATIONAL FEELING: PSYCHOLOGIST AND GUARDIAN

The Model J of these two types uses the following functions:

⌐ — **Relational Feeling.** Psychological environment, relations between people, morale issues, guarding of principles (I, Personality Program, for the both types).

▲ — **Potentiality Intuition.** Ability to assess inner capacity and potential of an object (II, Productive, for the Psychologist and III, Vulnerable, for the Guardian).

● — **Volitional Sensing.** Volitional pressuring, activeness, purposefulness, spatial control (II, Productive, for the Guardian and III, Vulnerable, for the Psychologist).

■ — **Practical Thinking.** Pragmatism, efficacy, expediency, technology (IV, Suggestible, for the both types).

THE PSYCHOLOGIST:
Feeling-Intuitive Introvert (FII)
⌐, ▲, ●, ■

General Appearance

The distinguishing feature of this psychological type is an impassive face and a vague look in the eyes, as if Psychologists (FIIs) are locked into themselves and only loosely connected with reality. Around the feeling subtype of Psychologists, an air of doubt and apprehensiveness can be felt, while the intuitive subtype is more open, friendly, and outgoing. If Psychologists dislike something, they may clam up for a while and «live through it». They know how to dress with style if they think about it, but may well ignore their appearance during periods of depression, which are not uncommon.

Type PSYCHOLOGIST

Characterization According to Strong Channel Functions

I. Personality Program Channel (⌐ — psychological environment, relations...)

While Psychologists promptly sense the complexity of interactions between people in any group, they restrain from revealing their own views. They try to smooth over any misunderstandings, always avoiding conflict: when a friend does not remember the Psychologist settling a debt, the Psychologist would prefer to quickly pay again, though quite confident in having paid the first time. Psychologists can not stand quarrels and would put up with a lot avoid them. They believe that «better a lean peace that a fat victory». If their patience comes to an end, they do not rage or yell. They simply erect a mental barrier between themselves and the offender — keeping a «stony» face, answering questions single-wordedly, and acting cold and official. If they hear that someone is in distress, Psychologists will go and try to help in any way possible. This can take the form of financial help or just lending an ear, taking some of the emotional burden upon themselves. People often come to Psychologists for a shoulder to cry on, finding them sympathetic listeners.

Psychologists cannot stand seeing someone hurt in front of them, especially a child, even if the child is being punished by his or her parents. In situations like this, they might approach the child's parents and talk to them:

> *You're teaching your child to be cruel! She will act the same way to you when you're old and weak!*

They will make sure the child does not hear this criticism. With their own children, Psychologists try to be fair: if they feel that they are in the wrong, they will ask the child's forgiveness.

If a Psychologist does something he feels proud of, then he childishly brags about it. Sometimes Psychologists are frank before strangers, sharing with them personal matters that they usually do not speak about. Later they may regret this and wonder why they did it.

Once they fall in love, Psychologists may keep their feelings concealed for years. However, if their torment is overwhelming, they may give up and confess to the object of their affections, most likely in writing. They do not care about the outcome, as long as their suffering stops.

II. Productive Channel (▲ — potential abilities, alternatives...)

Harmony in relationships with people is a Psychologist's life credo. To achieve this harmony, they search for true values in the world of inner-self and morality. From their youth, Psychologists make every effort to become the ideal they have shaped in their minds. Teenagers of this type often keep a diary, where they record their observations (mostly about themselves) and analyze their actions, harshly criticizing themselves for even the tiniest step away from the ideal.

A classic example:

> *A 15-year old high-school student, a Psychologist, had been saving his lunch money for a long time in order to buy the Swiss army knife which he wanted. When he had enough money, he realized that the knife was no longer being sold in stores, but there were two other Swiss knives: one that was even more expensive and attractive, and the other that was the same price, but not very appealing. What should he do? Wait and save up enough money for the better knife? However, he was set on buying a knife today. He stood at the window for a long time, staring longingly at the unreachable «treasure», but finally bought the cheaper knife. On leaving the store, he realized that the lady in the store had given him the other knife, the one he dreamed about. Here began his miseries. He stood for an hour at the door of the store, not able to return the object of his dreams. On the other hand, he felt morally wrong because he did not return the expensive Swiss army knife to the lady — that is, he deceived her. Finally, he settled on a compromise. He would keep the knife, but in the future, he would give back anything he got dishonestly right away, before he fell in love with it.*

From this example, it is obvious that Psychologists can mull for a long time over something anybody else would consider a given.

The priority of moral values can emerge in the Psychologists' life in the most unusual situations: for example, when the person they love prefers another, they may help their competitor get promoted. Psychologists consider harming their rival in this situation dishonorable.

When high ideals and moral values are determined by a genuine love of people, a person of this type can be very useful to the community as a teacher, preacher, counselor — a role model, in other words. As opposed to that, a Psychologist may also become an annoying moralizer and a bothersome lecturer.

Characterization According to Weak Channel Functions

III. Vulnerable Channel (● — volitional pressuring, activeness, survival in harsh competition...)

Psychologists take everything related to violence in any form very painfully. They judge their own actions in the categories of persistence and determination. They shape these qualities within themselves: they can work out a daily schedule, hang it on the wall, and systematically follow it. However, Psychologists tend to overexert themselves with vows approaching the point of selftorture. For example,

> *A ninth grade girl with acrophobia (fear of heights) struggled to strengthen her willpower, by forcing herself to walk over a river on a disassembled bridge, from which only a single 450-foot long metal rail was left*

> *(There was a newly built bridge nearby). When she achieved the goal, she decided to go back the same way, as it was not enough for her, though her knees were shaking from exhaustion. With great difficulty, pausing and looking up to fight dizziness, she made it from an island to the mainland, with a crowd of very agitated onlookers yelling at her. This endeavor nearly cost the girl her life.*

The Psychologists' slogan of self-perfection is «Do not what is wanted, but what is needed». While treating themselves this way (sometimes very harshly), Psychologists do not, however, press others, believing that everyone should improve upon themselves. They can not tolerate someone trying to force them to do something: they prefer to have nothing in common with people like this.

IV. Suggestible Channel (■ — pragmatism, efficacy...)

Psychologists lack a strong ability to work effectively, and this shortcoming is at odds with their battle towards self-perfection. As a result, they may force themselves to work «from dawn till dusk», exhausting themselves and wasting a lot of strength and energy where another person would do the same thing with a lot less exertion. The Psychologist gladly lets others teach him or her how to work more efficiently and feels grateful towards the person who does that. In this next example, a woman, a Psychologist, recalls:

> *I had a hard time trying to learn how to use my computer all by myself. Luckily, my 12-year old son is skilled in computers. Once, he showed me how to use the «Help» function when you don't know how a program works. It turned out to be pretty straightforward. Since that time I always use this function when I am uncertain what to do.*

In order to work productively, Psychologists require a favorable psychological atmosphere. They do not get along well with a boss who considers them incompetent. If their colleagues share their moral beliefs, they switch into work mode and are capable of working very productively.

Job Options

The best ways to make use of the Psychologists' abilities lie in the spheres of philosophy, religion, or missionary enlightenment. People of this psychological type can also be successful in education, and many FIIs feel pulled toward psychology. FIIs can also be found working in the field of art, though rarely as actors or actresses, as it is hard for them to perform in front of a large audience; rather, they are good at teaching in the Humanist field, or in colleges of the visual arts.

Famous FIIs: actors — Jeremy Irons; artist — Vincent Van Gogh; writers — Fyodor Dostoyevsky, Alexander Solzhenitsyn; politicians — Nicholas II — (the last Russia tsar).

THE GUARDIAN:
Feeling-Sensing Introvert (FSI)
⌐, ●, ▲, ■

General Appearance

The faces of Guardians (FSIs) with dominant Feeling are calm and impassive with nondes-cript features. Those with dominant Sensing, on the other hand, tend toward sharp, piercing looks.

Guardians are perfectly capable of standing up for themselves. In fact, they can unexpectedly and even ruthlessly put troublemakers in their place.

As a rule, they are outwardly sociable; yet internally they maintain a clear, psychological distance.

Type GUARDIAN

Characterization According to Strong Channel Functions

I. Personality Program Channel (⌐ — psychological climate, psychological distance, moral, relations...)

Ethical principles are essential for Guardians, they view obeying the priority of high moral values and the norms of civilized society as the only lifestyle acceptable for humans.

> *One day she strolled down the street and heard a young guy say: «What a sexy girl! I dream of having». She did not let him finish; she turned back and stared at him so furiously that the guy was struck dumb. She began to read him a lecture: «How dared you, what an outrage» etc.*

The age-old traditions and way of life formed by centuries of human history are especially important for Guardians.

Although people of this psychological type are rather emotional, they prefer to keep their emotions in themselves. They are rarely open, even with close friends. Stories like this one are typical for Guardians:

> *This winter, my former classmate Lily (an FSI) got married. When I found out, I couldn't believe it, as I'd never seen her in the company of any young man, much less a boyfriend. To the question of how long they'd dated before marriage, she answered, «About three years, not counting the years he served in the army.» I tried not to bring up the subject anymore because Lily didn't like talking about her personal life.*

If a sharp critical remark is voiced in front of them, Guardians might support it, though in a more gentle form- and if they argue against it, it is also without fervor. They try to avoid arguments and conflicts and are rarely intrusive.

Guardians have perfect memory for good deeds and wrongdoing. They remember any gift they have received:

> *There's the book (doll, shirt etc.) that you gave me once.*

If Guardians are wronged by someone, they try to avoid that person. One woman, a Guardian, remembers:

> *We swam far out into a lake, and one of my friends decided to play a cruel trick on me: he grabbed my leg. When we got back to shore, I tried to get away from those people as soon as possible. I still recall that occasion with a shade of antipathy.*

Sometimes this quality can transform into defiance.

> *A group of vacationers, including a man (Guardians) and a woman (Psychologist), were on the way to the beach when they stopped by a bench covered with ads for a theater. A young man — an advertiser for the theater — was passionately explaining the theater's new experimental style of plays. He earnestly promised that a bus would come to the resort for those who had purchased a ticket. For those who would miss dinner because of the play, tuna and chicken sandwiches and beverages would be served in the foyer. Some gullible people, including our couple, bought tickets. Of course, at the appointed time, no bus came, and everyone understood that they had been duped. The woman (Psychologist) was impressed by the abilities of the brave knight of fortune, telling everyone about what a show the man had put on, teaching everyone «not to be fools» — and for only $15!!!! The man (Guardian) impassively remained silent. The next day, he went to the local police station, showed them the tickets,*

and expressed his disappointment with «this outrageous fraud». He was thanked, and they promised to penalize this person, because the theater indicated on the tickets was, of course, not registered.

Guardians are equally strict in judging themselves, believing that there is no excuse for deceiving anyone.

In a company of people, Guardians easily define an informal leaders, and can call on their help if, of course, this is compatible with their ethical principles. They persuade people to work by convincing them to «have a heart», or «not let your fellows down», and the like.

II. Productive Channel (● — volitional pressure, spatial control...)

Throughout their life Guardians execute their moral program by using their sensing ability. They are insistent and demanding. They may tolerate pressure for a long time if they know it is unavoidable.

> *Here, for example, a young woman (a Guardian) is raising her son alone. By Russian law, she is entitled to time off to care for her child. However, she manages to work, get a good education «so as not to waste time», and take care of her elderly parents. She also has sleepless nights (her son is not yet even a year old). When asked how she does it, she smiles weakly and answers, «I'm used to it.*
>
> *She also manages to look appealing. She differs from many other people by her financial prudence and frugal lifestyle. During periods of inflation, she would use the broth from boiled vegetables for soup or leftover baby formula for her coffee. As a result of her thrift, she never runs out of money before payday.*

Another example:

> *A FSI man dreams of building a treehouse for his son, but does not have the necessary building materials. He searches for dead, dry trees in the forest, cuts them down to the right size, and drags them back to his garage on a sled. Over the winter, he collects nearly thirty logs, and makes boards out of them. Anytime he sees nails or any useful items lying around, he picks them up for future use. There is no doubt that, sooner or later, he will fulfill his dream, despite the lack of building materials.*

If Guardians believe their spouse is devoting most of their time to important and beneficial work, they might take all the household chores upon themselves. They are always oriented on helping in any way: to pull up a chair, to fill the refrigerator with food, or to take a jacket for his friend while going out.

Characterization According to Weak Channel Functions

III. Vulnerable Channel (▲ — potential abilities, conceptual alternatives...)

Guardians do not always grasp the actual abilities of people. Due to this, they may accuse their mate of cheating on them, without any real ground for such an accusation. They are poor at sensing changes in the society and economy. In the face of coming inflation, they may sell their summer home out of fear that it will be robbed, and lose almost everything as a result.

They become stressed if they must prepare for an important occasion — they anxiously examine everything that could go wrong, trying to be prepared for anything. Here is a Guardian confession:

> When I'm getting ready for a presentation or test, I totally lose control of myself. I begin to say things out of the blue, surprising everyone around me. During times like this, I am capable of putting things in odd places where nobody can find them afterwards. I might break dishes, or totally ruin everything I'm cooking if I'm expecting guests.

During such episodes Guardians feel relieved if somebody can share the responsibility with them:

> When collecting signatures for a petition, I can't sign as the first person on the list. However, if many signed before me, I would add my name with a free conscience.

Guardians put a lot of thoughts into analyzing their abilities, and often underestimate themselves.

IV. Suggestible Channel (■ — pragmatism, efficacy...)

Guardians are big fans of keeping everything orderly (● — strong function) and strive to do everything meticulously and thoroughly. It may take them a while to gather data, and then they would think at length about how best to do the job, and finally have all his energy exhausted and time used up on the preparation stage.

It is hard for Guardians to tell the principal from the secondary. They attempt to do everything at once as much as possible, and, as a result, feel incredibly overwhelmed at times not being able to commensurate their abilities with their plans. The idea of saving money sometimes becomes obsessive for them:

> One day I walked past my neighbor's cottage and saw him trying to saw a big log. He wanted to make a board for himself, instead of just buying it. «Why should I buy it when there are so many trees around fallen by the wind?» I doubted his ability to make a good board out of this stuff, and he later had to acknowledge I was right.

It is much easier for Guardians to do the job well if a partner can be found who can correctly and effectively organize the work for both of them. This psychological type is not competitive, and they easily retreat to a secondary role, where they find their vocation. In such cases the work may be much more efficient.

Job Options

FSIs are natural-born workers in the social sphere. Their abilities are excellently applied in medicine, in caring for the weak and impaired, in any economic activity. As a rule, FSIs love animals, are keen on farming, can serve with honor in the army, or become teachers and den leaders who care about how their students feel. They would not strive for a promotion but instead concentrate on his present day responsibilities.

Famous FSIs: actors — Leonardo Di Caprio, Michele Placido, John Travolta, Timothy Hutton, Robert De Niro, Nikolai Baskov; writers — Theodore Dreiser, Alexander Dumas (the son), politicians — Richard Nixon, Leonid Brezhnev.

STRUCTURAL THINKING: ANALYST AND STRUCTURIST

The Model J of these two types uses the following functions:

□ — **Structural Thinking.** Inventive structures, system, scientific theories (I, Personality Program, for the both types).

▲ — **Potentiality Intuition.** Capability to assess inner capacity and potential of an object (II, Productive, for the Analyst and III, Vulnerable, for the Structurist).

● — **Volitional Sensing.** Volitional pressuring, activeness, purposefulness, drive, spatial control (II, Productive, for the Structurist and III, Vulnerable, for the Analyst)

◣ — **Emotional Feeling.** Emotionality, open emotional influence, immediate emotional reaction (IV, Suggestible, for the both types).

THE ANALYST: Thinking-Intuitive Introvert (T I I)
□, ▲, ●, ◣

General Appearance

Type ANALYST

The most notable attributes of Analysts (TIIs) are a lanky body and a hollow-cheeked face, often with an elongated nose. They have a taste for casual attire; however, their suits are rather official and decent.

The Analysts' manner is, for the most part, gentle, reserved, and restrained — as long as their interests are not involved. When a matter that affects the Analysts is brought up, however, they may exhibit brusqueness that is surprising to those in the vicinity. Generally, they are guided in their actions by high moral values. They do not, however, reveal these values to others.

Characterization According to Strong Channel Functions

I. Personality Program Channel (□ — structure, system...)

Analysts are indeed analytical in their thinking. They strive to find logic in everything; to build a theory, system, or model. They enjoy creating new methods and various classifications.

An Analyst goes after ideas, not facts. Details are important to Analysts only when they concern the creation of a new system. They do not respect scientists who show «lots of emotion, but very little science». Analysts support every single fact they state, and demand the same of others:

> *Nobody gives a clear definition of what [metabolic] slag is as opposed to poison! Nobody tries to explain it — they [authors of popular books on fasting] call it slag, and that's it. At the same time, the physiology proves that poisonous substances are not produced in the body of a normal person with a healthy diet. (N. Amosov. Thoughts on Health. Moscow, «Fizkultura i sport», 1987).*

The pursuit of order and systematization is apparent not only in Analysts' work, but also in their hobbies. Analyst tourists may design their own backpacks to fit a personal definition of efficiency and pack them in special ways to optimize the space and weight.

In this next example, a woman tells a story about her husband, an Analyst:

> *After work, he fusses with his gladiolas all evening — he has almost 700 different varieties! He puts every bulb into a cloth bag, attaches a tag with a number on it, and records every variety by number in a special notebook. He even has a black gladiola — «Tobruc» — which is his special pride. In the summer, our apartment's like a flower shop, and there aren't enough vases for all the flowers. He doesn't want to sell them, though. A little while ago, he started making an electronic catalog — he photographs each flower with a digital camera, labels them on his computer, and organizes them by color.*

Analysts believe that in their social life, order and fairness are mandatory as well. Sometimes this belief turns into an over-enthusiastic pursuit of justice. They try to instill their own morals in their children. The daughter of an Analyst recalls the following incident of the 1950s:

> *He was the only person in our neighborhood with a bicycle. When he came home from work, we kids would line up, and he would take each of us around the neighborhood three times on his bike. It always upset me that he didn't give me any exceptions. I had to wait my turn just like everyone else, and he never let me ride longer than the other children.»*

Analysts can defend their principles over many years, in spite of the fact that their opponent may be in a higher position at work. Here is a story about an Analyst scientist:

> *For many years, he (an Analyst) argued with the director, who always placed profit above the institute's scientific interests on his list of priorities. The director, seeking a powerful ally and considering the Analyst's valuable scientific contribution, offered him a high-ranking position in the laboratory. The scientist declined the offer without hesitation. As a symbol of protest against this unprincipled act of the director, the scientist who brought fame to his institute retired at 60, at the peak of his Productive skills, and now works at home.*

II. Productive Channel (▲ — potential abilities, generalization, alternative concepts...)

Analysts can grasp the essence of phenomena, especially in the scientific fields. They easily comprehend new prospects and possibilities in any field. They are interested not only in their personal specialization, but also in related fields. Analyst's may also find unorthodox solutions to problems through the application of research from unrelated fields.

> *When my father, a mining surveyor, in the 1950s read a newspaper article about the invention of lasers, he quickly realized all the advantages of possible application of this method in mines, and in some years he implemented his ideas into practice.*

Having fully assimilated a piece of knowledge, an Analyst might present the material compactly and clearly, but not in a very captivating way. Students might call a teacher like this «smart, but boring».

Analysts do not use authoritative methods of management, preferring democratic methods.

Characterization According to Weak Channel Functions

III. Vulnerable Channel (● — volitional pressuring, spatial control, survival in harsh competition...)

Analysts can not stand being forced to do something. If they disagree with their boss's orders, they'll continue to argue their viewpoint and may get flustered, although they try to remain tactful.

It is hard for them to do dull, everyday tasks. However, they try to finish every thing they plan. They schedule not only their workday, but also their leisure time. For example, an Analyst may exercise daily and take a walk every evening before bed throughout whole life. Analysts prefer an orderly life; they cannot multitask. In clothing, Analysts stick to a «business» style, underlining their professional qualities more than their individual traits. They do not like garish styles and bright colors. Even females of this psychological type are reluctant to emphasize their sexual attractiveness (white circle).

IV. Suggestible Channel (■ — emotionality...)

Analysts are poor at sensing emotional subtleties. Due to this, Analysts behave very restrainedly, so as not to fall into a situation where they are badly oriented. This is why they prefer to keep their distance from others and dislike familiarity, intimacies, or whining. Analysts would rather offer concrete help, including monetary assistance, where needed.

> *I am not good in consoling other people; I tell them phrases which I myself consider unsuitable. When other people console me, it irritates me in the same way; I even perceive such words as formality rather than real compassion. In fact, I do not need such words, or, more precisely, it depends on who tells them. For this reason, I consider psychoanalysts to be quite useless people.*

Often, Analysts appear cold and unemotional. However, this is more a mode of behavior than the nature of this type. They can hide a rich emotional spectrum and great anxiety behind a mask of austerity. Analysts can carry resentment in their souls for many years and are reluctant to forgive an offender. They brighten noticeably when talking to an intellectual partner; they feel confident on this ground.

In relationships with the opposite gender, Analysts do not feel confident, are often afraid of showing their feelings, and are concerned about looking silly, even when talking to their boyfriend or girlfriend. One Analyst woman gives the following example:

> *I was walking on an old stone fence that I was afraid to jump down from, and my boyfriend (an Analyst) was too shy to even offer me a hand!*

Job Options

TIIs have all the traits necessary for a career in science. The ability to discover scientific laws and describe them clearly is important in any laboratory. The capacity to unravel complicated problems, visualize a problem in its entirety, and plainly describe the outcome makes the Analyst a good teacher and instructor.

TIIs often pursue careers where Productive skills are required: writers, composers, and artists.

Famous TIIs: composers — Sergey Rachmaninoff, Dmitry Shostakovich; ballet dancer Galina Ulanova, artists — Paul Gauguin; writers — Anton Chekhov; scientists — Rene Descartes, Marie and Pierre Curie, politicians — Maximilien Robespierre.

THE STRUCTURIST:
Thinking-Sensing Introvert (T S I)
□, ●, ▲, ⌐

General Appearance

Type STRUCTURIST

It is characteristic for men of this psychological type to have prominent cheekbones, making them look somewhat oriental. Mustaches suit them. Structurists' faces are calm and impassive. They appear rather stiff: the body usually turns with the head.

When socializing, they are gentle and polite. Structurists' homes are neat and well organized. They dislike others touching and moving their things.

Characteristics According to Strong Channel Functions

I. Personality Program Channel (□ — structure, system...)

Structurists possess a practical, business-like mindset. They try to classify and systematize everything around them and write all their information down.

> *When my younger sister became 4 or 5 years old, my parents gave me a box of slides to show her. Slides were mixed in total disorder, labels on boxes did not correspond to the contents, and I quickly got tired of it all. I classified the slides by boxes, numbered each box, and finally, created something like a catalog on cardboard cards. I still remember how happy I was of the outcome of my work.*

They create charts and graphs for everything, even self-improvement. In their own plans for the day, they prefer to specify time down to the minute. Every morning, Structurists make sure they are wearing a watch, as it is hard for them to get along without one. When settling the time and place for meeting someone, a Structurist specifies all the details. Upon discovering an ambiguity in their notes, they may underline it several times, and write a note in the margin.

In the field they choose for themselves, Structurists try to attain perfection and are very upset if someone outperforms them. In such situations, they may start working three times harder than usual, in order to remain the leader in their area of expertise. The effectiveness of Structurists business logics helps them to attain the goal, otherwise they could place themselves at the lower level of their own value system which is absolutely unacceptable for them. If the job concerns learning something new, they might study it for hours on end. If the Structurist is a student, his or her notes are always precise, clear, and thorough. Lectures are copied with neat handwriting. Structurists like all their headings to be exactly even, and the margin to be perfectly straight. Their personal notes to others are concise and coherent. Even letters to their boyfriend or girlfriend may seem like a well-organized report.

If Structurists begin something, they never procrastinate, but instead spread the work over the assigned time period, finishing well within the deadline. They know all rules, regulations, and instructions very well and do not mind sparing time to study them. Moreover, Structurists enjoy doing this and, when needed, apply learned rules freely and easily.

II. Productive Channel (● — volitional pressuring, spatial control, drive...)
Willpower, purposefulness, order, and discipline — these are the foundation of the Structurists' program manifestation.

> *My father tried to transfer his understanding of what and how to do to my sister and me. It is interesting to notice that he never explained why we should do this or that in such or such a way, he just told us how we needed to do that, in which order we should do things, in which form we should document results, etc. When my sister was unable to observe such a strict system, he began to yell at her and even castigated her. In spite of that all, he had warm relations with my sister up to his death; my sister always felt that she was punished not as a person but as a wrong-doer.*

They strive to reach as high a position as possible wherever they are, to dominate over the rest, rightfully thinking that with their ability to organize their labor and work hard, they deserve an important rank. Structurists' actions are always aimed at instating discipline and order. If a Structurist student is living in a dormitory, for example, he or she will make chore timetables, daytime schedules (watching a group TV show — Jeopardy, for example — also finds its way into this schedule) and hangs them up in the common room. Structurists demand that everyone follow the schedule. Moreover, if their attitude incites argument, or people begin making fun of them, Structurists might act rude or resort to fists.

If given an administrative post, Structurists can be quite harsh and even merciless. When not obeyed, they are given to making threats: «I'll find a way to force you to do this!»

Characterization According to Weak Channel Functions

III. Vulnerable Channel (▲ — potential abilities, unpredictable situations, conceptual alternatives...)

Structurists can't always comprehend other's abilities. Due to this, they are cautious and try to be on good terms with everyone. Those whose unique abilities stand out may aggravate Structurists because they do not fit neatly into the hierarchy that — according to the Structurists point of view — must be present everywhere. Poorly understanding people's individuality, they are inclined to put everyone on the same level. Structurists cannot always correctly evaluate the prospects of one possibility or another; and they tend to over-organize everything. Under their direction, projects are always completed in time, but research projects that require creativity and a non-standard mindset are not likely to prosper under the command of a Structurist.

IV. Suggestible Channel (◣ — emotionality...)

At a good psychological distance, a Structurist may seem like a gentle person — they rarely raise their voice and they abide by the behavioral norms accepted in society. However, it must be kept in mind that Structurists are veiled people, and rarely speak their mind. It may be hard for them to establish relationships with people (other than business relationships), including the opposite gender. In business, Structurists are sure that they are always right. Therefore, Structurists are capable of publicly making a reprimand that is right in subject, but offensive in form.

> *It is interesting to notice that my father, in spite of his strict approach even in relations with his family members, could drown in tears when watching sentimental Indian movies. He could not refrain from tears when he told stories from his past. Such sentimentality changed into outbursts of fury and indignation when he felt offended or «ridiculed».*

Job Options

TSIs are irreplaceable wherever strict conformance to rules, instructions, and detailed orders is necessary. They are ideal workers, for example, in pharmacies, where mistakes are unacceptable. They also make good workers in an assembly line or at a publishing company. TSI's can easily be mathematicians, programmers, or air traffic controllers. Often, service in the army is attractive to TSI's, because of the subordination, strict discipline, and clear responsibilities.

Famous TSIs: actors — Alain Delon, Murray Abraham, Nikita Mikhalkov; musisian — Sviatoslav Richter; composers — Johann Sebastian Bach; politicians — Saddam Hussein, Slobodan Milosevic, Joseph Stalin, Margaret Thatcher.

> **Note:** *In view of the fact that celebrities of this type contain so many dictators, we must emphasize here that there are no bad or good psychological types. A psychological type determines only the psychological structure. The level of the upbringing, morals, and the education of the individual all affect what that structure is filled with. Due to this, among the members of one psychological type, people who have nothing in common may be found. However, for all of them, the most characteristic feature is the aspiration for a certain system, which they are consistently trying to apply to their life, though the type of this system could be different.*

POTENTIALITY INTUITION: INITIATOR AND SEEKER

The Model J of these two types uses the following functions:

▲ — **Potentiality Intuition.** Ability to assess hidden capacity, potentials, create conceptual models, alternatives (I, Personality Program, for the both types).

⌐ — **Relational Feeling.** Psychological environment, relations between people, morale issues, guarding of principles (II, Productive, for the Initiator and III, Vulnerable, for the Seeker).

□ — **Structural Thinking.** Imaginative structure, system, scientific theories (II, Productive, for the Seeker and III, Vulnerable, for the Initiator).

○ — **Self-perceptive Sensing.** Spatial harmony, contentedness, well-being (IV, Suggestible, for the both types).

THE INITIATOR:
Intuitive-Feeling Extravert (I F E)
▲, ⌐, □, ○

General Appearance

Type INITIATOR

The Initiator's entire air implies some kind of gaiety. They don't restrain their emotions; their face is attractive thanks to the merry, dancing eyes. Initiators socialize easily and freely, they give the impression that they are always ready for precarious adventures, new acquaintances, and exciting encounters. Women of this psychological type love bright jewelry, sometimes they are set apart from other psychological types by plump «African» lips and widely spaced, spherical eyes.

Initiators easily create a group of friendly contacts around them, keeping pleasant, open relations.

Characterization According to Strong Channel Functions

I. Personality Program Channel (▲ — potential abilities, curiosity, conceptual alternatives...)

Initiators always try to be where they may find new prospects for Productive thinking and are always happy to take advantage of them. They quickly get tired of everything mundane and habitual. After just starting the blueprint for a promising new project, they may throw themselves into a new venture. Initiators perfectly understand people's motives and the essence of their relationships. They study anything new with delight. In company, they enjoy lighthearted pranks. Initiators begin any game with interest, they can easily become «a rocker, a break-dancer, a synchronized swimmer, a member of the beer-lovers' club» and stick to their assigned role for a while.

Initiators can marvel at a speaker's talents like nobody else, effortlessly inspire and energize people (for that matter, in order to solve their own problems):

> He (an Initiator) drove me home to sew these very pants. I worked on them for three days. They turned out to be a very extravagant pair. He thanked me from the bottom of his heart. After that, he disappeared for a while, and when I saw him next, the pants were a different color.

Initiators love extraordinary events; they always try to be there when they happen. When nothing new is happening, they may rearrange their furniture or even sell their house and take off to another city — not out of necessity, but just for a change of scenery.

II. Productive Channel (⌐ — psychological environment, relations...)

Initiators are good at understanding what others want of them, and happily satisfy the «social demand»:

> If you ask him (an Initiator) to stand on his head or draw a crocodile, or find a hard rocker's bracelet, he'll do it.

As they have little respect for accepted norms of behavior and the social hierarchy, they may sometimes look flippant. Women of this type, because of their cheerful personality, often seem easily accessible. However, if the situation becomes serious, they can give a decisive refusal.

In a familiar setting, Initiators are able to manipulate people's feelings, their sympathies and antipathies, readily displaying openness and cordiality, willingness to help, but they are not always reliable. Here is one person's story about an Initiator:

> I spent a lot of time getting to his (Initiator's) house at his request. He promised to wait for me. When I finely got there, his sister told me that Craig had gone to some party.

Initiators cover up these kinds of slips-ups by jokingly repenting. For example, they might fall on their knees in public and wail about their mistake. Naturally, everyone forgives them.

The irresistible urge to play pranks sometimes misleads them. For example:

> *A supervisor at a science laboratory, Leonid, had seen his graduate student very intently, holding a glass flask. He decided to relieve her of the burden. He came up behind her and clapped his hands above her ear, causing her to jump and drop the flask, which smashed into tiny pieces.*

At all costs, Initiators try to maintain friendly relations, searching for compromises when needed. They consider that friendship is more important than «holding on to principles». If they find themselves the CEO of the company and they must downsize it, they will try to find a well-paying job for those fired to minimize their distress.

Characterization According to Weak Channel Functions

III. Vulnerable Channel (□ — structure, system...)

Initiators are weak in administrative functions such as organization of work schedules, writing instructions, reports and the like. They have trouble restraining themselves to certain boundaries, their Productive nature does not accept anything predetermined. Logical analysis is difficult for Initiators. A girl of this type once said:

> *I am a smart girl; I do not need any thing to be explained more than three times!*

When doing scientific research, they cannot sit and meticulously do what is necessary, instead, they prefer to bounce a multitude of ideas off those around them. Any experienced scientist can remember at least one such colleague who often cheered his co-workers with the news:

> *Hey, guys! I've just had a splendid idea! I can even go pick up my Nobel Prize right now!*

Ideas, indeed, come in such profusion, that if only every one tenth is fulfilled, it is enough to defend dozens of PhD theses. This gives Initiators the reputation of talented researchers. However, they prefer that others test their ideas in their labs, as working independently on everyday tasks is a bore.

Initiators use a lot of imagination, creativity, and unorthodox approaches in their work. However, the inability to analyze things deeply is one of their shortcomings. Initiators may pay attention to the many minute details on the surface, while failing to grasp the big picture.

The irresistible tug towards everything new may involve the Initiator in a precarious venture.

IV. Suggestible Channel (○ — harmony, comfort, well being...)

Initiators lack interest in material possessions. It is not easy for them to keep things tidy, and anything requiring thoroughness and diligence quickly tires them.

It seems that George can get along without food just as long as he can. In a dormitory he never displays initiative in cooking, and moreover, often does not go to the cafeteria because of his laziness.

Initiators are not always sure about the necessity of one purchase or another. It happens that some object may attract them with its novelty and originality, and when bought, may lie uselessly in their house for a long time. In financial matters, Initiators are often imprudent. Money interests them only as a way to get new inspirations in life.

However, living for any period of time without paying attention to everyday problems is, naturally, impossible. Due to this, Initiators feel genuine gratitude to those who can take these problems upon themselves: for example, help them with financial duties, keep the house tidy, advise them on how to shop more advantageously.

Job Options

Due to their ability to adapt to a situation quickly and see new possibilities, this psychological type is invaluable as an entrepreneur, advertiser, or journalist, that is, wherever curiosity about anything new and the ability to win peoples» hearts are valued above all. Many IFEs successfully work as psychologists. Owing to their unorthodox mindset, IFEs may succeed in science, suggesting untraditional views on problems. However, scrupulous work and precise analysis is not for them.

Famous IFEs: composer Wolfgang Amadeus Mozart, actors — Whoopie Goldberg, Gerard Philippe, Andrey Mironov, Eldar Ryazanov, writer — Mark Twain, politicians — Nikita Khrushchev.

THE SEEKER:
Intuitive-Thinking Extravert (ITE)
▲, □, ⅃, ○

General Appearance

Type SEEKER

The most attractive feature of Seekers (ITEs) is their enthusiastic look, as if they are oversized children about to open a long-awaited present. Sometimes they walk with their hips and head slightly ahead of the rest of their body; Seekers are often preoccupied with something, causing them to neglect thinking about how their interests may affect or interfere with others' lives. The intuitive subtype is very dynamic — when engrossed in something, they may act heatedly and unthinkingly. The logical subtype is calm and reasonable.

Characterization According to Strong Channel Functions

I. Personality Program Channel (▲ — evaluation of potential abilities...)

Seekers have a knack for anything new that may be advantageous in the future. The spectrum of their interests is quite broad, going far beyond their occupation, ranging through medicine, religion, philosophy, avant-garde art, or even growing exotic plants in a greenhouse. Often they are attracted by ideas that seem too radical or groundless to their more practical colleagues. They try to use their knowledge to explain diverse phenomena. During fads where a new theory is popular, Seekers are generally ahead of others, and view this theory more objectively than everyone else, having their own deliberated opinion about it.

Upon achieving success, Seekers quickly forget the completed task; they hurriedly move on to new, more alluring projects.

Among the distinguished qualities of Seekers are acumen, intuition, and perception. They can go up to the chalkboard and immediately solve a problem they have never seen before. If they are questioned about how they did it, they might respond:

It's as plain as the nose on your face.

If they forget how to prove a theorem, they find a way to validate it right on the spot.

They have a knack for easily recognizing people's abilities. Here, one girl shares a story about her mother, a Seeker:

> *My mom can effortlessly recreate someone's character based on only my description of them. She manages to recognize character traits that I had no idea about, even if I had known these people for a long time. When I went to college, I described to her all the boys in my classes, and my mom focused on one of them. She said: «This is a wonderful person; you'll fall in love with him». At the time, I'd already fallen for someone else. However, in several months, my feelings changed; and in the end, I married the man my mother had «told me to». All this happened entirely without my mom's interference, but I often remember her prophetic words in wonder.*

Normally, the idea of profit doesn't interest Seekers: instead, they prefer to do things that are exciting for them.

> *All my efforts to discuss with Mike the price of the program we wrote were in vain. He was rather interested in the track our program will leave in the history of programming.*

II. Productive Channel (□ — system, structure, rule…)

Seekers love to ponder things — this trait is a characteristic part of their nature:

> *When we met, he surprised me with the profundity of his thinking. He deduced the laws of the universe and divided all of humankind into different categories.*

Seekers readily complete the unfinished theories of others, having studied in advance all available literature on the subject. They try to scrutinize all information they obtain and neatly organize it — reasons, consequences, and logical conclusions.

Seekers regard all dogmas with amusement, whether it is politics, a religious cult, or blind faith in any authority.

Members of this psychological type often initiate new scientific schools or projects, in which Productive spirit and administrative democracy dominate. This may emerge in traditional «round tables», where everyone has an equal right — whether they are fledglings or old hands — to present the most outrageous (even crazy) ideas. Seekers believe that the best method to convince people of something is scientific discussion — peer pressure is never used, even on the youngest and least experienced.

Characterization According
to Weak Channel Functions

III. Vulnerable Channel (⌐ **— psychological climate, psychological distance, relations…)**

For Seekers, the integrity and honesty of people hold great meaning. Their criteria for integrity are exceedingly high, as a rule. They are demanding, not only of themselves, but of those around them.

> *What does «sorry» mean?» asks Vlad (a Seeker), «What's done is done. With time, of course, it'll fade from memory, but if a person does something bad, then says «sorry», what's been done won't disappear! If a person deceives once, then what guarantees they won't do it again?*

Seekers try to judge people objectively. They consider it immoral to force anyone, no matter who it is, to do something that Seekers don't want to do themselves. In their opinion, every person is right in his or her own way.

Usually, Seekers are poor judges of what others think of them. Due to this, they study people new to them for a long time. Seekers don't want to be mistaken, so they cautiously wait until they have enough to go by. For the same reason, they behave restrainedly and officially with strangers. Sometimes they are not very diplomatic. Seekers can easily tell someone what they think of them in the way that they consider fitting. They may say to their girlfriend or boyfriend, «What are you, crazy?» and be genuinely surprised that she or he is upset.

IV. Suggestible Channel (○ **— harmony, comfort, well-being…)**

Seekers need advice in anything concerning their own well-being, health, and household organization. They do not pay much attention to the condition of their living area: whether it is tidy or messy. However, they are capable of sorting and cleaning their things from time to time, if the mess disturbs their life or work.

> *He is organically incapable of keeping his room in order. He seems to never care about disorder. When he wants to find something in his cabinet, it is easier for him to throw everything away from the drawers, then methodically rake out the heap, and then throw the things back into drawers chaotically, instead of methodically arranging everything.*

Generally, the financial situations of Seekers are not in the best shape possible. Often, anything they earn is spent immediately. However, they always have enough creativity (▲) to find a new opportunity to earn money.

Job Options
The best application of the ITEs' abilities is in fundamental science fields. Members of this psychological type are better than anyone else at launching new directions of scientific research through the Productive combination of sometimes very distant spheres of knowledge. Some ITEs can work just as successfully in business or commerce, most often in the manufacture of intellectual products, for example, a publishing company.

Famous ITEs: actors — Dustin Hoffmann, Edith Piaf; scientists — Aushra Augustinavichiute, Niels Bohr, Albert Einstein, Dmitry Mendeleyev, Andrei Sakharov, Seneca; musicians — Sergey Prokofiev, Mstislav Rostropovich; writer — Miguel Cervantes.

VOLITIONAL SENSING: LEADER AND ORGANIZER

The Model J of these two types uses the following functions:

● — **Volitional Sensing.** Volitional pressuring, activeness, drive, purposefulness, spatial control (I, Personality Program, for the both types).

⌐ — **Relational Feeling.** Psychological environment, relations between people, morale issues, guarding of principles (II, Productive, for the Leader and III, Vulnerable, for the Organizer).

□ — **Structural Thinking.** Imaginative structure, system, scientific theories (II, Productive, for the Organizer and III, Vulnerable, for the Leader).

△ — **Temporal Intuition.** Premonition, prediction, ability to perceive dynamics while they are developing, poetic nature, sense of the mystical (IV, Suggestible, for the both types).

THE LEADER:
Sensing-Feeling Extravert (SFE)
●, ⌐, □, △

General Appearance

The most distinctive feature of Leaders (SFEs) is their proud gaze. They look around as if they want to examine a potential battlefield before making a vital decision. Often, Leaders have round faces with short or «hawk» noses. Leaders are great optimists. They live with gusto; they are very invigorating, self-assertive, and sometimes even impertinent.

Leaders frequently wear stylish and impressive clothes. Women prefer bright and vibrant colors, red is one of their favorites.

Type LEADER

Characterization According to Strong Channel Functions

I. Personality Program Channel (● — volitional pressure, drive, influence...)

The most important thing for Leaders is being in control of situations, of the space around them, and being in the center of events.

> *People, animals, money, objects — everything is mine, I own and rule it. If I want to, I can give them to you, but I can take everything away, too!*

Leaders have very prominent leadership qualities like self-confidence and energy. If they are asked any question, even a very hard one, they answer assertively, without a shade of timidity. They easily understand the volitional qualities of people, and evaluate people's actions by their swiftness and boldness.

Here is how one man recalls his college classmate, Tina:

> *All the girls criticized her bossy tone, but, on the whole, they liked her. Tina was the leader of their crowd — she was the best in managing household problems, she was the best in academic skills, she was the most eye-catching and had the most scandalous reputation in relations with the opposite gender.*

The attention and activity of Leaders often switch from one object to another. Nevertheless, they hold on to one dream, which eventually comes true as a result of their persistent work in one direction.

> *If there are no problems in the company — he is bored. The problems must be created in order to be resolved and returned back to normal. Maybe, he was stimulated this way. He had to always play with his force.*

II. Productive Channel (⌐ — psychological environment, relations...)

Leaders effortlessly manipulate the people around them — their moods and desires. They like to be in the center of attention, aiming to infect people with their ideas and lead them. Leaders enjoy feeling authority and power.

Leaders are quick to argue, but just as quick to make peace, practically tugging the puppet strings that are clearly visible to them. Feelings are their strong point. They are able to reveal and demonstrate them. Leaders derive great pleasure from their influence over others:

> *Indeed, Caitlin accepts signs of attention even from the boys she dislikes, without explaining it. When she got a new boyfriend a while ago, they constantly argued, then made up again. Often, she said, «I left him for good». However, after a while they'd be together again.*

In their youth, education is not the major concern of Leaders. Romantic adventures are much more appealing. Leaders passionately get involved in these kind of escapades. They willingly share their love stories with friends, showing them photos of their boyfriends or girlfriends.

> *In her relations with young men, Mallory was keen on showing the initiative. Some people liked this, some were put off by it. I remember whenever she fell for a young man, she literally went crazy doing wild things. When she bumped into him, she would say horrible things.*

Their tug toward leadership forces Leaders to obtain a close friend to whom they can tell everything. In any company, they have at least one such close friend for moral support.

If an acquaintance, even a distant one, is in trouble, Leaders leap to the rescue without much thoughts. They may give up things they need themselves — items, money, or medicine. They absolutely cannot stand solitude — they lose all motivation for their actions.

Leaders usually display diplomatic abilities (of course, this depends on their cultural level).

They are capable of getting delight out of anything: night, stars, fireworks, going to the movies, horseback riding, and more.

Characterization According to Weak Channel Functions

III. Vulnerable Channel (□ — system, structure, rules...)

Logic is not the strongest trait of Leaders:

> *I love him so much, I hate him, —*

one college student (a Leader) said with perfect seriousness, not seeing the hypocrisy in this statement. It may not be easy for Leaders to determine what is needed and what can be sacrificed in a given system. They are reluctant to accept objective basic laws.

Leaders are prone to voluntarism. One can hear from them

> *If I don't like it — I won't do it!*

Sometimes Leaders cannot even give themselves a reasonable explanation for their impulsive actions. For example, here is a typical episode from a Leader's (a woman) life:

> *Sometimes she'd cheat on her boyfriend with one of her admirers, whom she detested. Afterwards she'd declare: «I have no idea how this could have happened! I'm so disgusted! I hope my boyfriend doesn't find out!»*

> *Leaders are annoyed by requests to «act reasonably». It is hard for them to bestow a logical ground for their measures — «I'm strong enough and I can manage it, that's all!» People of this type attempt to compensate the*

necessity to learn a lot of abstract knowledge («It's so boring and quite unnecessary!») with specific tricks.

Leaders are completely sure of themselves. Even if they are doing a job that is completely unsuitable for them, Leaders are still confident about completing it.

Once I wanted to hang a book shelf on my wall and had to drill several holes for nails. He (a Leader) entered the room, saw what I was going to do, grabbed a drill and began to drill without any preparation. I protested, told him that the shelf would hang lopsided — he did not care. It happened that the shelf really hung lopsided but the work was done quickly.

That is why Leaders take any tasks and jobs without the slightest hesitation. If Leaders are told that it is better to work on something else, they may simply not understand, «not hear» it, or not believe it.

IV. Suggestible Channel (△ — premonition, prediction...)

While seeing the outsides of people, objects, and events, Leaders cannot comprehend their inner meaning — Leaders sense well, but have poor ability of penetration into the fundamental nature of everything surrounding them. Due to this, it is hard for Leaders to judge not only others, but themselves and their actual place in life: as a rule, they overestimate themselves (▲ — a weak channel). It is hard for Leaders to plan their actions. In **the heat of battle**, they may reveal impatience and take unnecessary risks. Their assertiveness and enthusiasm can be applied much more successfully if there is someone nearby who can slow down their unnecessary speed, balance their chaotic moves with reasonable skepticism, and show them the true prospects of particular projects.

Job Options

For people of this psychological type, the most fitting professions are in fields where socializing with people at all levels is a must. This can be politics, service in the army (preferably in high-ranking positions), art, law, education, or secretarial work. SFEs should not work in scientific fields, especially not in theoretical fields.

They can easily find themselves in business and politics, due to their capability of persuading other people (let enviers call it manipulation!), being assertive and making good impression (in promotion of products, show business, etc.).

Famous SFEs: actors — Freddie Mercury, Elvis Presley, Elizabeth Taylor; Alla Pugacheva; politicians — Mikhail Gorbachev and his spouse — Raissa Gorbacheva, Mikhail Saakashvili, Gerhard Schroeder, Lech Walensa, Napoleon Bonaparte.

THE ORGANIZER:
Sensing-Thinking Extravert (STE)
●, □, ◧, △

General Appearance

Type ORGANIZER

Organizers (STEs) are generally recognizable by their willful mouth and rectangular chin, which is characteristic for the logical subtype. They often have a sturdy, well-built figure. Among the sensing subtype of Organizers, one can find elegant and appealing women; however, this psychological type is distinguished by their strong willpower.

In conversations, Organizers will often pause before answering a question in order to think about it and respond accurately. Organizers prefer plain and simple clothing, but some of them (mostly women) may favor an avant-garde style.

Characterization According to Strong Channel Functions

I. Personality Program Channel (● — volitional pressure, drive, ability to fight and to control space...)

Organizers' chief qualities are volitional pressure, resolution, and an unquenchable thirst for action and athletic fitness. They are people of accomplishment; they are not in the least interested in a life of contemplation.

Organizers strive to achieve their goals at all costs and by any means necessary. Organizers are resolute, decisive, and purposeful. Their interests are mainly practical. Quite often, Organizers are found acting as managers. While supervising, they work calmly, methodically, and without fretting or tension. When somebody contradicts them, Organizers firmly and persuasively defend their position, relying on facts to support their opinion. In conversation, they try to be respectful, but firm. Their tone of voice is usually lively, optimistic, and even. Organizers are good at judging and appreciating their employees' business qualities. Under their supervision, everybody feels well-placed and works with maximum efficiency.

If somebody on their team is insubordinate or obstinate, Organizers may be ruthless and intolerant, even about trivial things. Here is a typical example of such single-mindedness:

> *I really wanted to include rhubarb pie on a party menu, but my daughter, Tracy, cooked all of the meals according to her taste and categorically forbade me to «intrude with the pie». When she later found out that I had disobeyed, she became rigid and even more demanding, announcing: «If you don't stop this right now, I'll leave». The guests tried to ease the awkward situation by joking, but Tracy insisted on having her way and I had to comply.*

In this family, the daughter is an Organizer, while the mother is a Leader — not a fortunate combination. In similar situations, Organizers are capable of exhibiting «steely» notes in their voice and manner. If Organizers are set on a major goal, they may be remarkably vigorous, determined, and persistent, mobilizing their inner resources, for as long as needed to accomplish their mission.

> *When he is away, other colleagues often say, «Enjoy that the Fuhrer has not come back yet». In many years of working in this group no one of his people ever succeeded in making a career; people with initiative had to look for a different place.*

II. Productive Channel (□ — system, logical theories, rules...)

When trying to reach a goal, Organizers are capable of locating the best direction to focus their strength. They are logical and clear-headed in assessing any situation or in calculating the future results of one event or another. They expect fast and substantial revenue in any business, not believing in far-fetched projects. In management, when coordinating plans and schedules, Organizers make them public only when everything is scrupulously thought over and calculated. Organizers can quickly allocate responsibilities, suggest that a decision be made, a vote taken, or an issue deliberated. Organizers are able to manage big groups of people by clearly stating their goals and defining everyone's tasks. They maintain everyday control of progress and quickly step in when they deem it necessary.

When discussing business matters, managers (Organizers) listen carefully to every opinion in a discussion, but always have the final word on the issue.

Characterization According to Weak Channel Functions

III. Vulnerable Channel (⌐ — psychological climate, relationships...)

Organizers feel insecure when they need to perceive moods and the subtleties of people's attitudes towards each other and towards them. It is easier for then to give practical help to those who need it than to shed tears over them.

In difficult situations, Organizers are apt to be extremely reliable helpers and friends — they may buy a plane ticket, find a rare book, make an appointment with a renowned doctor, or help bake a cake for unexpected guests. When somebody has suffered a loss, Organizers will immediately organize anything necessary, without wasting words, in order to be of assistance.

Organizers demonstrate restraint in exposing their emotions (◣). They try to keep their daydreaming friends down-to-earth:

> *Don't get your hopes up. This still has to be thought through and calculated, so you might be disappointed later.*

Without showing signs of emotion, Organizers may help in a business-related subject, even if the subject does not involve their immediate job: arranging the repair of a broken copy machine, lending a hand in bringing a book to press, or organizing stress management courses. In order to resolve these kind of the problems, Organizers use their strong business logic (■).

Organizers do not like to talk about their own misfortunes, trying not to complain at all, although sometimes they might let slip some ironic remark about their wasted life (if they consider it such). At the same time, Organizers may be hurt if they feel a lack of concern from their family. What they do not realize is that such detachment is caused by their own independent lifestyle. One woman, an Organizer, complains:

> *I come home dog-tired, only to find out that he (husband) has no interest whatsoever in what I've been doing!*

Organizers, both men and women, feel uneasy about romantic relations. When the time comes, they cannot find the proper words to express themselves, being fearful to reveal their «weakness».

IV. Suggestible Channel (△ — presentiment, fantasy...)

Members of this psychological type often say they have excellent intuition, since they are good at predicting future events, generally being correct in evaluating them. This is true; however, the nature of such predictions is unrelated to intuition. Instead, the quality of these predictions is due to the fact that, more than anybody else, Organizers can judge a situation and calculate its outcome, based on reality.

In matters concerning mysteries and romantic or baffling images, Organizers feel left out, and possess deep gratitude towards anybody who can open up this *terra incognito* for them, making their lives richer and brighter.

Job Options

As indicated in the name of this psychological type, they are excellent organizers. No matter what field they work in — science, art, medicine — they will become managers sooner or later. Depending on their personal level, they may find themselves at the head of a small subdivision or an entire company. They can just as easily use their abilities in law enforcement or the army. STEs; competitive qualities also find good use in sports.

Famous STEs : actors — Sophia Loren, Sharon Stone, Jane Fonda, Tom Berenger; writer — Aurore Dudevant (more known as George Sand); fashion designer — Coco Channel; politicians — Peter the Great (Russian tsar), Vladimir Lenin, Georgy Zhukov (one of the leading generals of the Soviet Army during WWII); Soviet rocket scientist — Sergei Korolev.

EMOTIONAL FEELING: PERFORMER AND ENTHUSIAST

The Model J of these two types uses the following functions:

■⌐ — **Emotional Feeling.** Emotionality, open emotional influence, immediate emotional reaction (I, Personality Program, for the both types).

△ — **Temporal Intuition.** Premonition, prediction, ability to perceive dynamics while they are developing, poetic nature, sense of the mystical (II, Productive, for the Performer and III, Vulnerable, for the Enthusiast).

○ — **Self-perceptive Sensing.** Spatial harmony, contentedness, well-being (II, Productive, for the Enthusiast and III, Vulnerable, for the Performer).

□ — **Structural Thinking.** Imaginative structure, system, scientific theories (IV, Suggestible, for the both types).

THE PERFORMER: Feeling-Intuitive Extravert (F I E)
■⌐, △, ○, □

General Appearance

Type PERFORMER

For Performers, a somewhat irresolute lower face and flaccid, sometimes capricious mouth is characteristic. The narrowest, most «aristocratic» faces belong to Performers. In socializing, they are a bit theatrical, with over-exaggerated emotionality, they always watch for the audience reaction. If Performers feel that they are being observed in an unfavorable situation, they become tense, looking at the observer out of the corner of their eyes, noting reactions to their remarks and actions. Numerous performers are members of this psychological type.

Characterization According to Strong Channel Functions

I. Personality Program Channel (⬛ — emotionality...)

Performers are people of very intense emotions. They easily become excited, and just as easily deflate. Everything, down to dismal weather, affects their mood. Such people easily fall into pessimism:

> *I always wake up in a bad mood.*

Performers may spend the whole day in a gloomy mood and they love to be pitied; they feel hurt if nobody pays attention to them. If a Performer asked someone a question and did not get an answer right away, they might unexpectedly become enraged:

> *What, did you swallow your tongue?! Or do I mean so little to you that you won't even answer me?!*

If Performers meet somebody new and interesting, they immediately become livelier, and charged with energy. In company, people of this type are cheerful, and often witty. They greatly depend on what others think of them, especially their boss. Even a chance remark may throw them into a deep funk for a few days.

Even though Performers' emotions are very pronounced, most often, they unwind by spilling their emotions onto others, which allows them to quickly forget everything and calm down. However, if the offense is especially upsetting, Performers take it like a blow and give the offender the cold shoulder, if not forever, then for a long time. Sometimes, for several days in a row, they can act despondent , showing everyone how offended they are, but not explaining why — they let others fret and try to figure out what they did wrong. When asked what is wrong, they may expressively keep silent, or unexpectedly answer with something like:

> *Why are you interested all of a sudden? You don't really care about me!*

Performers are very good at sensing the emotional condition of other people, they may immediately sympathize or offer help, showing great generosity.

They are experts in art, music, and literature. Here is an example:

> *After watching movies, especially those made by Tarkovsky or Fellini, we always hurried to get Victor's (a Performer) opinion about them. His commentaries were surprisingly correct, and we immediately comprehended anything that was vague earlier.*

People of this type may be very eloquent, even if their main profession is far away from the field of linguistics. They are capable of writing long, rather captivating, interesting letters — this is not difficult for Performers.

In love, Performers demonstrate very intense emotions, dignity, and resourcefulness in ways of showing a passion.

II. Productive Channel (△ — premonition, prediction, imagination...)

The wild imagination of Performers help them to capture and hold others' attention and to lead people.

> He was always full of productive ideas. He was a good artist; when he had to implement his new project, he made everybody around him serve his objective. Other people gladly found him necessary materials, posed for him and even fed him...

The Performers can devote themselves to a Great idea, especially if they believe it to be noble and unique. The opportunity to demonstrate their own distinctiveness is what stimulates and inspires them. They are adept at predicting future events:

> Even at the time tidings of the «Kursk» submarine had just barely arrived, Victor said about Putin's trip to Spain, 'What's he doing? He needs to go to Murmansk immediately, not to Europe, he won't be able to deal with the situation! It'll get out of control!' At the time, this seemed to me a groundless warning, but now, I see how right he was then.

Performers show an equally useful talent in predicting the actions of any acquaintance, especially a close friend. Often Performers consider it their duty to warn others of possible danger.

> In the first 15 minutes of my acquaintance with a new person I quickly realize how I can offend this person and how I cannot. Usually, when I have such opportunity, I watch the person for about 15 minutes, and then, if I decide they are not important to me and I will lose nothing if a break the acquaintance, I will begin to balance on a brink and watch their reaction.

Performers are good at reading people's faces. Even by looking at a photograph, they may say what to expect of the person.

People of this type are not inclined toward compromises and patience, and due to this, they are reluctant to be engaged in an activity in which these qualities are a must, for example, teaching children. They may be harsh and demanding in their families.

Characterization According to Weak Channel Functions

III. Vulnerable Channel (○ — spatial harmony, contentedness, well-being...)

Although Performers are confident in their own abilities, they feel unsure in the field of everyday problems, health, and well-being. Not being good at understanding their bodies' needs, Performers may either run to the doctor constantly, or not get medical help until they collapse.

People of this type love comfort, but are not adept at creating it. Here is what a Performer's daughter tells about her mother:

> *Every Sunday, my mother would start sorting her things. By the evening, they were piled in heaps on every chair, couch, and recliner in the house, and, even though I was very busy, she would ask me, «Sweetie, please help me to clean this up». This is how every weekend was. She even needed a helper on weekdays, so she could give him or her orders, ask a favor, or, to somehow express herself.*

Performers are immaculate and fastidious:

> *When entering the elevator, Constantine never used his finger, but always a key from his apartment to push the button. When coming to a friend's house for dinner, he thoroughly studied the dinnerware, and as a rule, if he did not find it spotless, went to the kitchen and washed it himself.*

Performers cannot stand physical distress and pain. They like to travel, but only if conditions are comfortable.

Performers are inferior at picking out suitable clothing and, realizing this fact, they ask for help. However, those of them who are art experts, are able, on the contrary, to select superb color combinations for their apparel.

IV. Suggestible Channel (□ — imaginative structure, system…)

Performers do not like to multitask, which is explained by the attention they give to their work. The slightest distraction from the task at hand might seriously annoy them. Even doing something tedious, they still prefer to complete the job with diligence. Performers are directed by their own emotions and are not attentive to logical reasoning. They are capable of validating any statement with equal conviction, if they believe in it or the statement is essential to them. Even in situations where Performers recently stated the opposite, they still might argue for it with the same fervor.

In general, Performers like to prove themselves in the intellectual field, demonstrate their competence in philosophical matters, and talk about abstract topics. In order to demonstrate their versatile knowledge, Performers collect different facts from various sources, so when the opportunity arises, they can display their intelligence in social chit-chat.

Sometimes this psychological type works in the fields of mathematics or physics. In these situations, people will say about their work:

> *It's rather art than science.*

Naturally, strong intuition, rather than logical structure–which they use to create unorthodox approaches–is apparent in their studies.

Job Options

The most effective application of the FIE's abilities is in those fields where it is necessary to captivate an audience. This is, most often, the theatrical stage. FIEs are also excellent artistic and inspirational teachers. Many FIEs are attracted to politics because they enjoy manipulating the emotions of a crowd. Often, they have a gift for literature, music, arts, or dance. A proficiency in sensing others' emotions brings some FIEs into the field of psychology.

Famous FIEs: actors –Fyodor Chaliapin (singer), David Copperfield, Charlie Chaplin, Audrie Hapburn; dancer — Rudolph Nuriev, artists — Iliah Repin; writers — Victor Hugo, William Shakespeare; politicians –Osama Bin Laden, Adolf Hitler, Ronald Reagan, Leo Trotsky, Russian tsar Ivan the Terrible.

> **Note:** *I would like to once again remind the reader that a psychological type is only a structure, and the structure of the Performers is such that they are able to win people's hearts and souls. While one person may manipulate crowds and start terrible wars (Hitler), another may bring out the most refined and vibrant emotions in people (Chaliapin).*

THE ENTHUSIAST:
Feeling-Sensing Extravert (FSE)
◣, ○, △, □

General Appearance

Enthusiasts (FSEs) differ from other psychological types by their congenial gaze — they look as if they want to relate some good news. Indeed, they do try to share good news when possible. If they are not in a hurry, they will stop to ask acquaintances how they are doing, or invite them to dinner.

Many Enthusiasts have a light, dancing, ballet-like gait. They are very sociable and love giving presents.

Type ENTHUSIAST

Characterization According to Strong Channel Functions

I. Personality Program Channel (◣ — emotionality...)

Life for Enthusiasts is an emotional ocean in which they are swimming. They control this space, collecting its energy internally and then returning it outwards tenfold. Enthusiasts are adept at sensing others' moods, and they are rarely in a bad mood themselves. For example, this is how an Enthusiast is perceived by his friend:

> I've never really seen Eric upset, worried, or angry. He's always cheerful and friendly; you can see it on his face that he is happy.

Enthusiasts feel that their mood has to be treated almost like a material possession: it must be kept in good condition and shared with others; and if it is bad, it must be hidden. They consider ruining a person's mood to be almost like robbing them. Even in tough situations, they keep their humor:

> Why do I need to buy two new shoes? The sole fell off only of one of them, I can save some money on the other one!

They approach their work the same way:

> Today we were finishing up some work with glassblowing that had taken several days. The demanding work nearly drove us crazy, and when we

> *only had a few minutes to go in order to finish, one of my absent-minded technicians came in and smashed it all to bits. You know, just from absentmindedness! If not for my young age — I'm not even 60 yet, you know — I would have had a heart attack. The glassblower was so astonished that he couldn't even find a comforting word to say to the poor woman.*

People of this type cannot stand rudeness and outright insult. In such situations they instantly retort in the same fashion, even if their boss is standing in front of them. They may even say something they will regret later.

If Enthusiasts are infected with some idea, they stick with it until the end. From youth to old age, they may keep the same hobby, like fishing with their friends or music, with which Enthusiasts might become fascinated. They may get so caught up in this hobby that they begin to perform in public or compose ballads, even in old age.

II. Productive Channel (○ — harmony, comfort, well-being…)

As a rule, people of this type have a romantic and artistic nature. They can effortlessly create a comfortable and attentive social atmosphere. A colleague of an Enthusiast shares her impression of him:

> *Aaron is always very polite. He's always tactful while socializing, giving the impression that, at any minute, he'll break into a medieval-style bow. If I come into his laboratory, he will stand and offer me his chair, he will never sit when I'm standing…oh, if only all men were like that!*

> *He always has a lot of ideas where to go — to play pool, to make BBQ etc. He is insuperable in organizing leisure.*

Love and tenderness are always present in Enthusiasts' lives. If Enthusiasts must break up a relationship, they will do it at the very last minute, hoping that everything will be settled without their interference, as they cannot stand having the responsibility of a ruined relationship on their shoulders.

If someone asks Enthusiasts for help, they try not to turn the person away, even if they are working on something important at the moment. Here is one example:

> *Once, my daughter and I couldn't get into our apartment, until Ryan (an Enthusiasts), who was extremely busy writing his new book, came out and helped us open the door. He bustled around for a long time, using odd things to try to pick the lock, and explained to me what he was doing every second. When he opened the door, he said, «If this happens again…(he gave me instructions) — or, better yet, just come get me and I'll help you».*

Enthusiasts always dress with taste; and if their clothing is plain, they spice it up with some kind of elegant accessory:

> *Kevin wears the avant-garde style, however, he never goes to extremes. He just wears loose pants and shirts and flat-soled shoes; but, for the sake of style, he puts on red socks and, sometimes, a bright hat.*

Characteristics According o Weak Channel Functions

III. Vulnerable Channel (△ — premonition, prediction…)

Enthusiasts hardly sense the passage of time, so they dislike instability and prefer to know specifically what they are going to do tomorrow, and the next day, and after that. They hate wasting time, and because of this are always busy. It is hard for Enthusiasts to evenly distribute their strength and decide what is most important at the moment, and what is of secondary importance. This causes them to bustle a lot, trying to do everything at once.

In public relations or administrative issues, Enthusiasts may be inefficient and sometimes even behave naively due to their inability to comprehend undercurrents or concealed matters, as in the example below.

> *Imagine, when invited to a fundraising dinner, he (an Enthusiast) requested a limousine! Doesn't he know he was not supposed to do so?*

In another example, an Enthusiast recalls:

> *A lady from Human Resources called me and asked to attend an annual ethics course. What's the point of taking it every year? I already know everything in the first place.*

As Enthusiasts have a bad sense of time's passage, they may seem like conservatives, solve a problem very straightforwardly, or waste a lot of time and energy on doing something that has already been done — «reinvent the wheel», so to speak.

IV. Suggestible Channel (□ — imaginative structure, system…)

The distinctive qualities of Enthusiasts — a short attention span and emotionality — interfere with fully thinking actions at work. Enthusiasts are guided by their fluctuating moods; it often happens that they do not «look before they leap». At the same time, they may immediately realize their mistake, and admonish themselves for it. Later on, emotionality gets the better of them, and the cycle starts all over again.

> *One day, after a sleepless night in the lab, she handed the synthesized substance to the customer. The latter found that the whole work was in vain — the temperature indicated in the instruction given by her boss was wrong. She was furious — a lot of time, work and materials were lost.*

She told the boss everything she thought about him, organization of work in the lab in general, employee wages, benefits, and finally declared that she wanted to resign, even though the resignation was extremely disadvantageous for her at that specific moment — she was paid a very small severance at the time of economical collapse in Russia.

As a rule, Enthusiasts reach their goals as a result of furious activity rather than careful planning.

Job Options

The strengths of FSEs are best applied in the field of human services. They enjoy working with people: they love to explain, help, advice, and graciously answer all of their clients' demands, no matter what. In business, jobs related to the acquiring of contacts, product design, and advertising are generally the best ones for FSEs. Doctors, teachers, and wonderful actors can be found within this psychological type.

Famous FSEs: writer — Jules Vernes, composers — Johann Strauss, Aram Khachaturian, Charles Aznavour; dancer — Mikhail Baryshnikov; archaeologist — Heinrich Schliemann.

PRACTICAL THINKING: ENTERPRENEUR AND PROFESSIONAL

The Model J of these two types uses the following functions:

■ — **Practical Thinking.** Pragmatism, efficacy, expediency, technology (I, Personality Program, for the both types).

△ — **Temporal intuition.** Premonition, prediction, ability to perceive dynamics while they are developing, poetic nature, sense of the mystical (II, Productive, for the Enterpreneur and III, Vulnerable, for the Professional).

○ — **Self-perceptive Sensing.** Spatial harmony, contentedness, well-being (II, Productive, for the Professional and III, Vulnerable, for the Enterpreneur).

└ — **Relational Feeling.** Psychological environment, relations between people, morale issues, guarding of principles (IV, Suggestible, for the both types).

THE ENTERPRENEUR: Thinking-Intuitive Extravert (T I E)
■, △, ○, └

General Appearance

Entrepreneurs' faces look like they belong on a poster; often, they are of a rectangular shape, have an open, optimistic appearance, and a courageous facial expression. Members of the thinking subtype are very dynamic and enterprising. People of the intuitive subtype are calm and hardworking, and gladly help people if asked.

Enterpreneurs are big fans of hikes and journeys, even risky ones. Many members of this psychological type can be found working in dangerous professions — for example, policemen, firefighters, or stunt-doubles.

People of this type are not too good at understanding the intricacies of style; they may often wear the same clothes (most likely of an athletic style) for long periods of time. Enterpreneur women are not always able to pick out matching makeup and accessories for themselves.

Type ENTERPRENEUR

Characterization According to Strong Channel Functions

I. Personality Program Channel (■ — Pragmatism, Efficacy, Planning of Processes...)

Enterpreneurs are hard workers, toiling relentlessly and gladly. Their thoughts focus on theories that might be helpful in real life. Their desks are often piled with popular scientific magazines. They are apt to look at any job from the pragmatic point of view. Here is a story related by a Enterpreneur's friend:

> I remember how his grown-up son told him (an Entrepreneur) that he wanted to build a tree house. Within a few days, he gave his son papers with a set of instructions. Among the papers was a very detailed blueprint of a tree house. It looked like a professional had drawn it. There was also a list of the materials that should be used and their quantities; plus where it would be best to buy them. There was also a sheet of paper with the heading «Instructions». These were step-by-step directions of how to build the tree house. At the end were the date and his signature.

Entrepreneurs orient themselves well in the field of business. They never pass up an opportunity to earn some money; and usually they do not care how money is earned.

Even in everyday life, Enterpreneurs try to make use of their Productive, practical thinking. An Enterpreneur's wife shares a story about her husband:

> Long ago, he invented his own technique of making dumplings. He flattens a large piece of dough, puts it on a cutting board of his own construction, and adds the meat. He covers all of this with another piece of dough and rolls it up — there are 50 dumplings all at once. Commercially available dumpling maker sets appeared a lot later.

Enterpreneurs are capable of taking risks. However, the risk is always thought through and calculated beforehand. With their business partners, they prefer to practice fair play. As a rule, Enterpreneurs fulfill their promises and hate to be in debt.

II. Productive Channel (△ — premonition, prediction...)

A balance of practicality and romanticism is characteristic for Enterpreneurs. Their introverted intuition is materialized in inexhaustible fantasy, and in their ability to combine mentally the events and facts that are impossible to combine in the real world. They can calculate the optimal solution to any problem; they can often find a way out of an extraordinary situation.

> He was a legendary personality in the hospital; nurses, doctors and patients told how he puting all his effort as long as he could to avoid sur-

gical intervention, and to protect his patients' health. When he operated on them, he always invented new improvements, like methods of inserting needles or fasteners for bones, in order to accelerate the recovery of a patient. Several times, I attempted to ask him about his work and his life, but he always gave me the same answer:
— I cannot sleep until I hold in my hands something new and invent something new to do with this thing ...

Enterpreneurs plan everything ahead of time, creating charts not only at the workplace, but of household tasks, too. Unlike Professionals (sensing type), they perceive time management not only as vital necessity, but as their field of creativity (I — ■, planning of processes is supported by II — △, sense of changes in time). Precision and punctuality have special meaning to Enterpreneurs. If their partner is late for a meeting, Enterpreneurs feel the need to reprimand them. Enterpreneurs do not like to act without preparation; even leisure time must follow a schedule. Here is a typical example.

We were celebrating New Year's at her (an Enterpreneur) house. It was a congenial company in a stress-free, cozy environment, but, nonetheless, everything was planned out: under the tree, there were labeled presents for each guest, and funny jokes on the wall met the eye. Even when she invited me, she gave me strict instructions about what New Year's stuff to bring and what games to prepare.

Enterpreneurs love to experiment, whether in theory or in practice. Elements of a game are present in the way an Enterpreneur approaches things.

When doing important business work, Enterpreneurs search for innovative technologies, wishing to take advantage of all their opportunities. Enterpreneurs are focused on overcoming obstacles (●).

Characterization According to Weak Channel Functions

III. Vulnerable Channel (○ — harmony, comfort, health...)

Enterpreneurs are not very sure of themselves in anything that concerns well-being, everyday necessities, or aesthetics. Sometimes they try to employ fantasy and initiative even in these fields, but their actions may cause bewilderment:

Her outfits always gave the impression of an odd combination of untamed fantasy and bad taste. She might have decorated her dress with plastic circles and triangles, worn extravagant, blouses on the very edge of propriety, or dressed in checkered pants that made her look like a clown. She wore all these clothes like a model demonstrating examples of elegance and harmony. She often sought approval from her acquaintances: «Look what a great outfit I thought up!» Her house was decorated with the same weird style.

If an Enterpreneur lacks such self-confidence, his or her clothing will most often have an athletic style.

Members of this psychological type can easily deal with the discomfort of their surroundings, but only if it does not harm their health. Striving towards a healthy lifestyle, Enterpreneurs love to vacation in the wilderness — often hunting, hiking, scuba diving, mountain climbing, or camping. They keep their gusto even in old age:

At 75 years, he has not lost his taste for life — he planted a garden where he works with great interest and knowledge, drives a car excellently, does all the men's work around the house, and is not afraid of life's problems. In the company of friends, he is a bubbly and witty person, who enthusiastically throws himself into any game and livens it with stinging jokes aimed at his opponents.

IV. Suggestible Channel (⌂ — psychological environment, relations between people...)

In socialization, Enterpreneurs try to stick to the norms of behavior accepted in the group they are in. Their moral criteria are rather high. They are fans of risky hikes where everyone is tested, not only for physical fitness, but also for trustworthiness, friendship, and the ability to help friends in need. They value these character traits above all others. In everyday life, Enterpreneurs try to keep balanced, calm relations with everyone. They believe that there are no benefits from arguments and it is better to discuss all misunderstandings and try to work out a reasonable compromise.

Enterpreneurs cannot stand silent demonstrations of discontent; in such situations they calmly say, «Explain what's wrong. Let's sort everything out instead of being offended». The intricacies of idle chit-chat in the higher circles of society do not interest them.

Job Options

The ability to sense the slightest changes in a situation, quick reactions, initiative, and practicality in combination with creativity make TIEs great business persons and managers. They are capable of effectively organizing work; this ability especially applies to unstable situations. TIEs easily find their place in any research organization — they are excellent experimenters and inventors. Their love of romance and journeys brings many of them to work as geologists, marine biologists, in polar exploration teams, as test-pilots, or even as astronauts. They may also successfully use their abilities in military service or law enforcement, most often in active duty.

The ability to bring elements of a game into work attracts children, so they are often favored teachers.

Famous TIEs: actors — Jack Nicholson, Jean Paul Belmondo, Julia Roberts; cientists — Lev Landau, Enrico Fermi, Richard Feynman, Robert Wood, businessmen — Bill Gates, George Soros; politicians — Tony Blair, John Kennedy, Franklin Roosevelt, Fidel Castro, Boris Eltsin; writer — Jack London, Russian fieldmarshal Alexander Suvorov.

THE PROFESSIONAL:
Thinking-Sensing Extravert (T S E)
■, ○, △, ⌐

General Appearance

Type PROFESSIONAL

People of this type usually look trim and athletic; their straight bearing is similar to that of military officers. Their motions are well coordinated, although somewhat constrained. The Thinking subtype is assertive and dynamic, tending to have outbursts of irritation, especially when people who try to teach them are incompetent in their eyes. The Sensing subtype is rather calm, open and benevolent. They also tend to outbursts of irritation but not as often as the Thinking subtype. However, in communication with strangers a Professional (TSE) avoids familiarity, demonstrating politeness and good manners.

In dressing, Professionals prefer business or classical styles; they are very neat and often conservative.

Characterization According to Strong Channel Functions

I. Personality Program Channel (■ — pragmatism, efficacy, planning of processes...)

Professionals are very active people; they hate idle time. Even their spare time is nothing but an opportunity to do something useful. Men of this type consider it their duty to achieve necessary life standards for their family by honest working and not by shady transactions. When Professionals start something, they start it because of its usefulness and not out of curiosity, and necessarily strive for completion.

The only serious reasons Professionals can accept are facts. They underpin their statements with facts and require the same from other people. When they begin a new project, they methodically collect all the information about the upcoming enterprise, analyze all possible option, and act only once they understand all the details. Men of this type are fond of various tools:

My younger brother sleeps with a drill he got as a gift!

They strive for perfect quality in everything they do. This quality is easy to notice in people of this type from their childhood.

My 12 year old son decided to make a model of a wooden church in Kizhi (an old Russian town) from safety matches. His work lasted for 2 years, and I was impressed by his accuracy, how he was pleased to methodically paste in each match into his project.

Professionals like order. Each tool (including forks and spoons) has its own proper place.

My son was always displeased when I mixed knives, spoons and forks on a drain board after washing. He wanted to put them separately, forks with forks, spoons with spoons, likes with likes.

Such people tend to methodically plan and consider upcoming events, analyzing the details.

Before Alice starts to do anything, whether knitting or sewing, she accurately prepares her workplace, tools and other accessories. When she has to do something she does not know perfectly, she collects a lot of information about the task and then performs it methodically and with concentration. When she fails, she repeats her work from the beginning.

The main criterion of competency for a Professional is logical consistency.

When we watch a movie — especially Bollywood — he always makes severe remarks about illogical actions of a hero or the whole plot; in spite of indignation of other TV watchers, he cannot hold back from such criticism.

II. Productive Channel (○ — harmony, comfort, health...)
This type is strong in their ability to combine ideally utilitarian aspects of life with esthetical ones. They like things of high quality and create comfort around themselves.

Alice's room delighted everybody's eye. When she purchased a new nice thing, for example a checkered blanket or a lamp, she examined it with pleasure and liked to remark on its merits.

Professionals have the same attitude towards their work:

Paul is accurate in his work, he is a born perfectionist. When he writes new software, he cares not only for its working and functionality but for its handy interface as well.

As managers, Professionals want to create appropriate working conditions for their subordinates — they believe that only providing such conditions gives them the right to be exacting.

A Professional is a good expert in the material world. Women of this type manage to buy not too expensive but practical things which other people notice only after such a purchase is done. They notice and remember details of clothes, and have good sense of form and fashion, even when they are not fashion designers.

Very often people of this type are physically strong and hardy. Being ill is so unusual for them that they are frustrated when it happens and do not expect such events or like premonitions of such kind. Here is what a woman tells about her husband, a Professional:

> *It is a torment for me to treat him; when a medicine does not bring a quick result in a day or two he believes it should be thrown away. In such cases he becomes irritable and bad-tempered.*

Characterization According to Weak Channel Functions

III. Vulnerable Channel (△ — premonition, prediction...)

Professionals negatively perceive any uncertainty. Being people of a sensing type, they want to know exactly what will happen tomorrow, in a month, in a year. Uncertainty is hard for them and makes them nervous. Weakness of their intuitive function is the reason for their conservatism, and their unwillingness to accept innovations; for example men of this type may prefer the same style of suits for decades (women of this type are less conservative in regard to clothing). They methodically analyze previous mistakes in order to not repeat them in the future. There are very stable in their devotions and habits, do not like unexpected changes, and are mistrustful towards everything that can change their life (for example, new jobs or new places of residence).

Time management is their pride and their greatest problem. They try to plan everything, and deviations from their plans unsettle them. Being extraverts, they have a lot of plans and agreements; however, being sensing types, they spend too much time on details and run the risk of losing tempo and flexibility, and of missing the opportunity to be at the right time and place.

> *When the time for college examinations comes, Michael begins to methodically read all his records and manuals, and spends a lot of time reviewing each theorem. It often happens that he manages to read a greater part of the necessary materials, which he knows perfectly, but can get low grades on exams when questions concern the part of the material he did not have time to read.*

IV. Suggestible Channel (⊔ — psychological environment, relations between people...)

Being incompetent in the world of feelings, they try to keep to certain established styles of behavior; as a rule, they prefer the image of a polite and reserved person.

However, this style is used rather in communication with strangers, while family members, in their opinion, should understand their true attitude towards them without such «ceremonies».

> *Sometimes I make critical and not very delicate remarks about my wife's outfit. She feels aggrieved, but I do care and thus cannot avoid commenting. In general, when I criticize, I never want to offend, but I find it necessary to argue when I believe my point of view is true.*

Professionals demonstrate their attitude by helping in everyday family activities, spending a lot of time with children, caring about the professional growth of their spouses — in other words, they show their care by deeds and not by words. At the same time, they do not like to look too «soft», like by saying words of sympathy. In unpredictable psychological situations, Professionals prefer to do something helpful instead of saying words of love or sympathy.

> *I had not seen Alec (a Professional) for a few months; I missed him so much and prepared myself for our meeting. However, my trip to see him failed, and I was so sad that I burst into tears. When he met me, he was irritated by my tears, he became more and more cold and restrained and at the end of my visit our relations were very tense. The day before my departure he suddenly said that he would bring me home by car: 400 miles to my city and 400 miles back. Well, I could easily buy a train ticket instead! Of course, he made this decision in order to prove his love to me.*

Job Options

The best opportunity for TSEs to apply their capabilities is in practice-oriented activities; for example people of such type are capable of organizing a production and of caring about its high quality, and of being good managers. However, to achieve that, they need stable situations and a predictability of events.

TSEs may be very good in military service — it is a good place to apply their inborn capabilities, or work as police officers or lawyers. Very often, TSEs are successful in professional sports, especially in team games.

Famous TSEs: actors — Sean Connery, Bruce Willis, Konstantin Stanislavsky; scientists — Peter Kapitsa, Ernest Rutherford; politicians — Helmuth Kohl, Angela Merkel, Nursultan Nazarbayev, Peter Stolypin (a progressive Russian politician before WWI), famous soccer goalkeeper Lev Yashin.

Part III
INTERTYPE RELATIONSHIPS

The most fruitful and promising part of socionics is its hypothesis of intertype relationships; it allows not only analyzing but also prediction of relations between individuals with certain psychological types. This hypothesis is based on the presumption that the informational structure of psyche of each of the 16 types imposes definite restrictions on the communication with other types of people. These restrictions depend not only upon the type of the individual himself but also on the psychological type of his partner. In other words, we can say that the two informational systems can either cooperate or function «in anti-phase,» suppressing each other.

How does this happen? How do people of different psychological types communicate with each other? Let us consider an example of relationship between a Professional (Thinking-Sensing Extravert) and an Epicurean (Sensing-Feeling Introvert).

Interaction between the Professional
(Thinking-Sensing Extravert)
and the Epicurean (Sensing-Feeling Introvert)

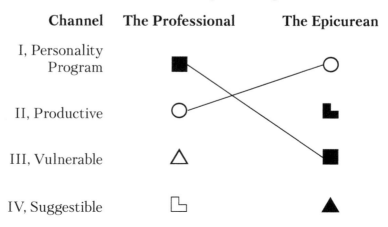

Channel	The Professional	The Epicurean
I, Personality Program	■	○
II, Productive	○	◪
III, Vulnerable	△	■
IV, Suggestible	◱	▲

It is important to note that throughout the act of communication, information relevant to a certain psychological function of an individual is always accepted by the channel occupied with the same function of another individual. For example, a Professional (■ ○) makes a renovation in his house using his strong Practical Thinking ■ (Channel I). Epicurean (○ ◣) can perceive all his actions only through his own Practical Thinking ■ function. This information exchange is illustrated on a scheme above by the line that links Practical Thinking in Channel I of the Professional with Practical Thinking in the Channel III of the Epicurean. Analogous link, related to the Self-Perceptive Sensation, exists between Channel I of the Epicurean and Channel II of the Professional. What does this mean in practice? Strong signals from Channel I of the Professional are accepted very poorly by the weak Channel III of the Epicurean: to him, it feels as if someone has treaded on a sore with a heavy boot. In contrast, the Professional does not perceive information from Channel I of the Epicurean as painfully because the same function occupies his Channel II, which is also strong.

Interaction between two other pairs of functions, Feeling (◣ and ◳) and Intuition (▲ and △), is weak because these pairs have different «vertnesses.» From this superficial analysis, we can draw an important conclusion: the relationship between The Epicurean and The Professional implies a unidirectional negative influence on the former by the latter.

Analyzing in the same way all possible combinations of links between channels of two individuals belonging to different psychological types, we will obtain 16 types of intertype relationships. As an example, Table 3.1 lists all 16 types of relationships for the Sensing-Feeling Extravert (a Leader).

Table 3.1.
Part 1. Relationships between types with opposite «vertness»

111

Table 3.1.

Part 2. Relationships between types with the same «vertness»

9	10	11	12	13	14	15 and 16

1. **Duality or mutual complementation** (The Leader–The Critic).

2. **Semi-duality or incomplete complementation** (The Leader–The Romantic).

3. **Contrast** (The Leader–The Epicurean).

4. **Illusion** (The Leader–The Craftsman).

5. **Mirror** (The Leader–The Guardian).

6. **Conflict** (The Leader–The Analyst).

7 and 8. **Supervision** (The Leader is supervised by the Structurist and supervises the Psychologist).

9. **Identity** (The Leader–The Leader).

10. **Kindred** (The Leader–The Organizer).

11. **Super-Ego** (The Leader–The Seeker).

12. **Collaboration** (The Leader–The Initiator).

13. **Activation** (The Leader–The Entrepreneur).

14. **Quasi-Identity** (The Leader–The Enthusiast).

15 and 16. **Social request** (The Leader is requested by the Performer and is a requestor for the Professional).

Now let us consider the intertype relationships in the same sequence as they are presented in Table 3.1. We need to notice, however, that all the proposed interaction models are valid only ceteris paribus, i.e. when both interacting individuals are «equally developed». Therefore, we will not consider situations where, for example, Channel I is much weaker in one individual than in another. Strong differences between the individual' levels of self-actualization go far beyond the limits of our abstract analysis.

1. DUAL RELATIONSHIP (Mutual Complementation)

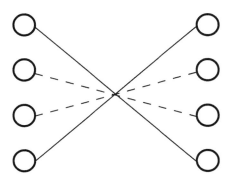

Duality is a relationship of mutual complementation. Since the scheme of duality is identical for all of the 16 types (the link between the Channel I and the Channel IV connects like functions, while the link between the Channel II and the Channel III joins disparate functions), the illustration (as well as for all other types of relationships) does not include specific functions but rather shows links between identical functions with solid lines and links between differing functions with dotted lines (where applicable).

As we have noticed, human psyche is asymmetric, there being no one whose psychological functions have been equally developed. It would appear reasonable that any of us should have the most pleasant relationship with a person whose psychical asymmetry complements ours. Socionics calls such a complementary partner a *dual*. Information from a dual's strongest Channel I comes to the partner's Channel IV, which ignores pressure/criticism and willingly accepts help. Thus, information from a dual is perceived as a support, positive correction, and readiness to facilitate solution of a complicated task.

The link between the partners' Channel II and Channel III is shown as a dotted line. This kind of interaction does not allow partners to put pressure on each other, because, on the one hand, Channel II is not as strongas as Channel I, and, on the other, because of the different «vertness» of interacting functions.

Table 3.2.
The Four Quadras

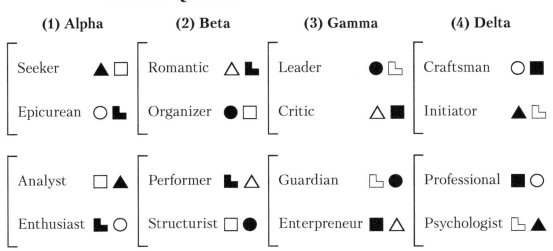

Functions in the first two Channels of dual types are mutually complementary. Two dual pairs with the same set of strong functions make a Quadra. Quadras are referred to by letters of the Greek alphabet: Alpha, Beta, Gamma, and Delta.

What are Quadras? These are unusual groups. They contain 4 types having none of the 4 Jung's criteria in common. They are based on a different principle than similarity—namely, on the principle of complementation between their strong functions. It's like a key and a lock: they look quite differently, but their shape «complements» each other. Quadras represent something more than just a sum of psychical properties of all the 4 types: as a result of such interaction, they acquire some new extra properties not peculiar to any of these 4 types when those are considered separately.

Detailed consideration of the four Quadras goes far beyond the topic of this book.

Strong functions of any two pairs belonging to the same Quadra are the same (two extraverted and two introverted functions); only their order is reversed. Each one of these four functions is necessarily present in Channel I of one type in this Quadra, thus providing the necessary help to the other three types. In this way, the Quadra provides better cooperation than a dual pair. This is a group of optimal psycho-physical self-regulation: all its members receive a feeling of mutual understanding and support from other members.

Psychological types in a dual pair differ one from another in Extraversion vs. Introversion, Thinking vs. Feeling, and Sensation vs. Intuition. However, Rationality or Irrationality coincide. This means that duals complement each other in three characteristics, while the coinciding Rationality or Irrationality determines the similarity of their vital tempos. Each of the Quadras contains one rational and one irrational dual pair.

Duals usually perceive each other as reliable partners in any undertaking, whether that be work or family life. Independent statistical research performed by various socionists (Augustinavichiute, report of 1982, published 1998; Boukalov, Karpenko and Chikirisova, 1999; Filatova, 2000) show that dual pairs prevail among the most stable family pairs. People usually say about such pairs:

> *How I like being in their house! It is so cozy, and they seem to never quarrel. When the husband does something wrong, one look from his wife is enough to make him understand—and vice versa. She notices at once when he dislikes any of their guests or when a conversation becomes too noisy.*

This observation illustrates how duals support the weak functions of their partners' Channel IV with the same functions in their strong Channel I.

Table 3.3 below provides a detailed description of Channel I and Channel IV functions for each of the dual pairs. Note that each type's Channel IV requires exactly the kind of help that is produced by their dual's strongest Channel I.

Table 3.3.

**Duality as Complementation
between Strong and Weak Functions**

The Seeker		The Epicurean
Intuitive-Thinking Extravert		**Sensing-Feeling Introvert**
Channel I ▲		○ **Channel I**
Burning curiosity for everything new, inquisitiveness; unpredictable behavior; creative excitement; ability to recognize essence under the surface		Focus on well-being and physical comfort; ability to create comfortable and pleasant feelings; good cooking capabilities
Channel IV ○		▲ **Channel IV**
Need for support in everything that concerns health, well-being, and leisure activities		Seeing the surface rather than the essence; need for help in foreseeing potential outcome of actions and in evaluation of his/her potential capabilities

The Analyst		The Enthusiast
Thinking-Intuitive Introvert		**Feeling-Sensing Extravert**
Channel I ☐		⌐ **Channel I**
Analytic thinking, classification, generalization; striving to understand general principles, for creating a model of the world systematization		Cannot live without people and communication with them; creates atmosphere of an emotional feast for self and others; charges people with enthusiasm and good tonus
Channel IV ⌐		☐ **Channel IV**
Reserved and cautious in relations with others; poorly understands emotional nuance; fears looking obtrusive and therefore prefers keeping a distance in communication		Difficulty in prioritization and information structuring; often makes precipitate decisions based on emotions

The Romantic
Intuitive-Feeling Introvert

Channel I △

Romantic daydreamer who easily forgets reality for the sake of dreams which are the source of inspiration and understanding life

Channel IV ●

Follower, not leader; difficulty manifesting initiative and willing himself to do something or to undertake responsibility for something

The Organizer
Sensing-Thinking Extravert

● Channel I

Volitional action; irrepressible lust for activity; sportive tonus and decisiveness; capability of not missing initiative and winning in competition

△ Channel IV

His/her courage very often over-weighs caution. Sometimes he lacks inspiration: «For what sake am I doing this all?». He cannot self-inspire because of his mistrust for everything vague, mysterious and unearthly, and is thankful to those who can inspire him

The Structurist
Thinking-Sensing Introvert

Channel I □

Finds a stable structure (e.g. organization) and obeys its laws; systematic and concrete thinking

Channel IV ◩

Poorly understands others' emotional reactions; secretive; often meets difficulties in communication

The Performer
Feeling-Intuitive Extravert

◩ Channel I

Brilliantly manipulates other people's emotions, just like a conductor conducts an orchestra; affects people using a broad range of feelings

□ Channel IV

High emotionality warps judgments; logic subjugated to emotionality

The Critic
Intuitive-Feeling Introvert

Channel I △

Holistic and systematic perception; foreseeing of far-going perspectives and upcoming problems, sometimes excessive caution

Channel IV ●

Inertia; difficulty mobilizing for necessary actions; need for outward stimuli and inspiration

The Leader
Sensing-Thinking Extravert

● **Channel I**

Irrepressible purposefulness; haste; self-confidence; leadership capabilitie

△ **Channel IV**

Impulsive, prefers making future with his/her own hands instead of trying to predict it (and thus often ignores even the most obvious dangers); good tactician but usually bad strategist

The Enterpreneur
Thinking-Intuitive Extravert

Channel I ■

Efficient working; dynamism; budgeting efforts; separating the wheat from the chaff

Channel IV ⌐

Weak understanding of nuances of intonation and of other people's moods; thankful to those who can unobtrusively help correct relations with other people

The Guardian
Feeling-Sensing Introvert

⌐ **Channel I**

Has a quick eye of people's moods, and their relationships; moralist; observation of traditions and rituals

■ **Channel IV**

Preparing to work and work itself require effort; difficulty separating the wheat from the chaff; and establishing a balance between plans and possibilities

The Initiator
Intuitive-Feeling Extravert

Channel I ▲

A talent for sensing promising opportunities, for discovering talents of people, for understanding the essence of matters

Channel IV ○

Weak sense of own body and needs, problems with household organization, carelessness in financial issues, preference for delegating such matters to somebody else

The Craftsman
Sensing-Thinking Introvert

○ **Channel I**

Dominance of the sensual world, harmony, balance and expediency in everything, esthetics combined with practicality, good sense of own body, capability of creating comfort and well-being

▲ **Channel IV**

Weak understanding of hidden processes and of one's own hidden capabilities, gratitude to those who help to understand his own iniquity

The Professional
Thinking-Sensing Extravert

Channel I ■

Dominance of reality; need for people to submit to objective laws; importance of efficient work, high quality products, observation of law and order

Channel IV ⌐

Poorly understands nuances of feelings; holds to accepted behavioral conventions; confused by non-standard ethical situations; difficulty in changing habits

The Psychologist
Feeling-Intuitive Introvert

⌐ **Channel I**

Sensitivity to others; obedient to moral norms; capable of empathizing and of establishing a good psychological climate; an expert in traditions

■ **Channel IV**

Insecure about ability for efficient work; excessive amounts of time and effort spent in achieving necessary results

Note. *You may have noticed that manifestations of the same functions are slightly different for neighboring types — compare for example the Volitional Sensation function in the Channel I for the types Leader and Organizer. This different «smack» is caused by difference of functions in their Channel II, which is not considered in this table.*

2. SEMI-DUAL RELATIONSHIP (Incomplete Complementation)

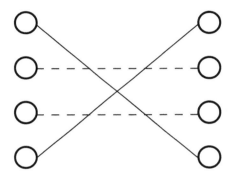

Interaction between Channels I and IV for semi-duality is similar to that for duality. However, compensation between the Channels II and III is absent. For this reason, when semi-duals meet for the first time, make joint plans, or arrange activities, everything works just as smoothly as for duals. However, when semi-duals start to put their plans into practice, they hit the same snag, although somewhat differently (they have the same function in the Channel III, although of a different «vertness»), and therefore their mutual assistance is not sufficient. The lack of compensation may result in mutual disappointment in the case of close and long-term relationship.

Isaac (Romantic), being aware of expected inflation and worsening of economic conditions and meanwhile daydreaming of a village resort, proposed to his wife Olga (Leader) that they invest their savings into the purchase of a garden plot and build a house on it. His wife agreed and immediately began to act—chose a good place with a river, a forest, and a road nearby. In spite of the notorious Russian bureaucracy,

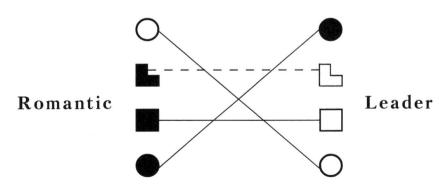

Romantic   **Leader**

she used all her eloquence and energy to obtain the necessary appro-vals. However, when the construction of their house started, she often acted impulsively, even illogically (III − □), which resulted in finan-cial losses and waste of time, while the husband did not apply much effort to holding up his end of the project (III − ■). This made his wife reproach him with You drew me into this affair and now have washed your hands of it!

3. CONTRASTIVE RELATIONSHIP

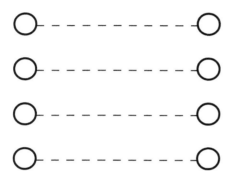

Usually people have a successful informa-tional exchange when they have common com-munication channels. However, in the case of the contrastive relationship, identical communication functions are completely absent. Partners have the same functions in the same channels, but of different vertness. This means that partners look at the same problems from different standpoints, e.g. one of them pays more attention to external factors while the other relies more on his subjec-tive opinion and vision. As a result, their commu-nication is rather superficial, as if they speak different languages. It is very difficult for them to have a common business because they lack common understanding even in smallest things and fail to coordinate their actions.

In the beginning such partners attract each other by the novelty of their approaches. They seem somewhat mysterious to each other. Unfortunately, marriages between contrastive partners are not exceptionally rare. No wonder that such families are not happy; their relationship is often at stake and almost inevitably results in a divorce.

In the following exaple, the husband Stanislaw is a Craftsman, and his wife Nathalie is an Organizer.

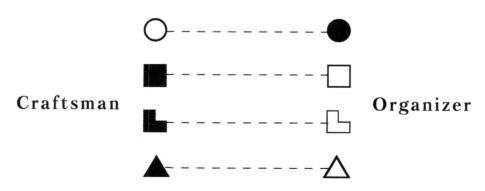

Craftsman   Organizer

The Craftsman: «She always commands: eat this, do not touch that (I — ●). When I visited my neighbors, it looked quite differently — the neighbor's wife offered juice and asked whether I liked it—I always appreciate such an attitude (I — ○). It seems that I will never find a common language with my wife. She prefers to pressure (●, □), and I have to retreat in order to protect my independence (○, ■)».

The Organizer: «I have a lot of problems at work. I am so worried, and he never cares about my being so upset» (The Organizer's Channel III — ⌐b). He is always silent and cold like a fish, dead to all feeling (The Craftsman's Channel III — ◣)».

4. ILLUSIONARY RELATIONSHIP

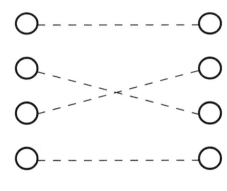

In an illusionary relationship, due to the indirect link between the partners' Channel II and III, similar to the dual relationship, they can render very good assistance to each other. However, the Channels I and IV are not complementary. This means that partners usually have good relationships in non-serious undertakings and leisure activities. In these instances, support from the Channel II of one partner to the Channel III of the other is sufficient. The weakest channel, Channel IV, remains unprotected, and the functions in the strongest Channel I are the same but of a different «vertness» and thus extinguish each other. The partner's strongest function seems to be not really important (*«I can manage it myself in a different way»*), and his weakest function looks especially miserable: such a partner seems to be not too serious, although easy to communicate with, a kind and pleasant person, with whom it is nice to spend time together but not someone whom

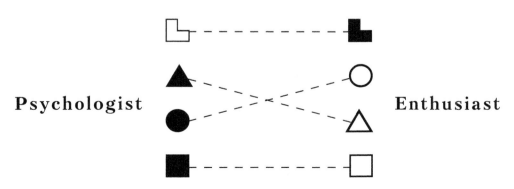

Psychologist **Enthusiast**

would be attractive as a business partner. Such a relationship may be quite comfortable in family life for those who place psychological comfort first and foremost.

Here is what Boris (a Psychologist) telling about his wife (an Enthusiast):

> *The relations between my wife and me are wonderful; our marriage has lasted for 30 years. She takes care of the household brilliantly, and she is a very good cook — our friends often visit just to taste her cakes. And finally, she never grumbles; she is always cheerful and affable.*

This is a good description of how The Enthusiast supports her husband's vulnerable Sensing function.

5. MIRROR RELATIONSHIP

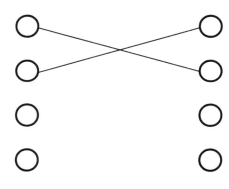

Partners in this relationship are very similar—they are both Thinkers or both Feelers, both Sensers or both Intuiters. However, one of them is an extravert, while the other is an introvert, and one is rational and the other irrational. Such interaction is characterized with active information exchange between their strongest functions (Channels I and II). The thoughts and reasoning of one of them (Channel I) is exactly what the other puts into practice without much ado (Channel II). They can learn a lot from each other, although sometimes they feel tempted to teach each other. Yuliya (Craftsman) tells about her friendship with Irene (Professional):

> *I enjoy working with Irene. She immediately notices contradictions in my calculations and solutions and insists on reviewing the draft over and over again from the very beginning. It makes me a bit tired; however, problems solved this way leave no doubts about the correctness of their solutions. When we make common appointments, it means that we will go for sure due to her insistence even though I begin to invent excuses. I cannot attend the lecture because I have to write my annual report and do not have necessary books... I should go to the library but these books have probably already been taken out, so we would be better off going out for some ice-cream... (○). Finally, I am tormented by remorse and promise to attend at least the second half of the lecture. One day we went shopping together. She liked a pair of shoes; they were nice and not expensive. In my opinion, if you like something, just buy it immediately (I — ○, II — ■).*

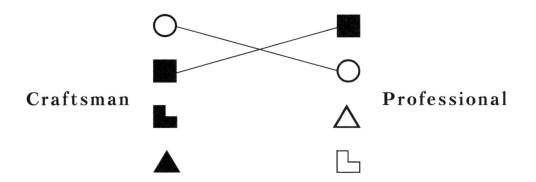

Craftsman   Professional

However, Irene tried on 4 other pair and finally chose a pair that I did not like. I asked why she had chosen just that pair. The main criteria for her were that they were durable, their stitch was accurate, and finally, their color matched her wardrobe (I — ■, II — ○).

In the mirror relationship, the strong functions of one partner do not touch the weak functions of the other, and the vulnerable Channel III remains unharmed. For this reason, «mirror» partners are unlikely to have conflicts with each other.

6. CONFLICTIVE RELATIONSHIP

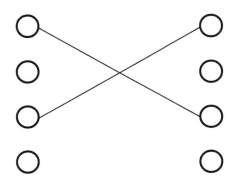

Information from Channel I of one partner hits the vulnerable Channel III of the other, and vice versa. For this reason, this relationship is not pleasant. «Conflicting» partners may like each other and mutually sympathize only from a far psychological distance. Each of them is attracted by the partner's strongest function, especially because in this sphere they lack self-confidence and are vulnerable to criticism. However, when partners attempt to come closer to each other, they both feel strong pressure on their weak function and automatically increase communication distance

Victor (an Analyst) speak about his wife (a Leader): «It's intolerable! I have the feeling that she alone occupies the whole room, always giving orders and instructions, and everything results in a hollow rush! She first does something and only then thinks!»

In this case, The Analyst obviously feels strong volitional pressure on his vulnerable sensing function.

> *Here is what, his wife, (a Leader), says: «It's such good weather outdoors. Birds are singing. I am sitting at the open window and enjoying the sun and young green leaves, and he (The Analyst) is sitting in the next room with closed curtains and a lamp on, solving his problems and reproaching me for my laziness. In his opinion, I will inevitably fail my exams!»*

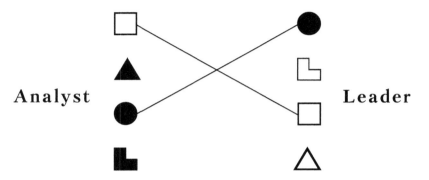

In this case, The Leader feels unhappy with communication with such a partner because it puts pressure on her weak Structural thinking function.

Of course, such people cannot achieve harmony in close relations, e.g. in a family. However, when they keep a distance in communication (e.g. being members of the same club), their advice to each other is often fruitful. They can even keep a «distant friendship» for many years when they respect each other.

7, 8. RELATIONSHIP OF SUPERVISION

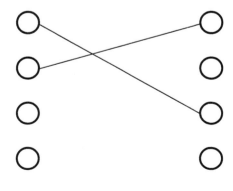

We have already talked a bit about this relationship in the beginning of the chapter. Compared to the conflictive relationship, it is asymmetrical, which makes it even more painful. The partner who feels pressure in his weak Channel III is more vulnerable. In Socionics, this person is called a Supervisee and the partner who affects his vulnerable function is called a Supervisor. All the 16 types are in such relationships with each other that each one is someone's Supervisor and in turn is «supervised» by another type. There are four supervision loops altogether, each including four types.

Table 3.4

An example of a supervision loop

Channel	The Seeker	The Structurist	The Leader	The Psychologist	The Seeker
I, Personality Program	▲	▢	●	◳	▲
II, Productive	▢	●	◳	▲	▢
III, Vulnerable	◳	▲	▢	●	◳
IV, Suggestible	○	◤	△	■	○

Table 3.4 represents one of these loops. Looking at this table, you will understand how these types «supervise» each other, and will be able to build three other loops.

It is important to emphasize the asymmetry of this relationship: the Supervisor, feeling no psychological pressure from of a Supervisee, can approach her up to a dangerously close distance. Partners in the conflictive relationship are more careful about «hurting» each other, because psychological pressure is reciprocal.

How is this relationship perceived by the Supervisee? As a rule, people tend to speak out on subjects that attract their attention, especially when these issues concern their strong functions. Other people may be either interested in this information or indifferent to it, depending on their curiosity. However, a Supervisee is extremely sensitive to casual remarks of her Supervisor, because they touch his/her vulnerable Channel III *(in contrast to the conflictive relationship, these remarks are expressed in his/her language because the function in the Supervisor's strong Channel II is the same as that in the Supervisee's Channel I).*

The Supervisor suffers from this relationship in his own way: simply not understand why whatever he says to his Supervisee offends him, irritates him or even awakes his aggression. The Supervisor perceives his partner as somewhat rude, irritable, shrinking into himself all of a sudden, making him creep about on tiptoe. «I just tell it like it is without any intention to offend her!» the supervisor says. «Why does she react so sharply?»

> *Student Boris, a Seeker, is lying on his bed—staring as usual at the ceiling and inventing a model of the Universe. His roommate Sergey, a Structurist, is preparing for an upcoming exam. Sergey is irritated by Boris, who*

> *always succeeds on exams in spite of his seeming laziness. Sergey perceives this fact as rankling injustice. Suddenly Sergey breaks the silence in exasperation, «Stop sloughing off and clean up your dresser! Can't you see the mess here?»*

> *«So what?» Boris replies calmly. He simply cannot understand why Sergey is always so angry and irritated in his presence.*

What is going on is that Sergey is irritated by Boris' inapproachability, his careless freedom of mind, his far-reaching intuition that allows him to see the final result without working at it, something that is quite impossible for a Structurist. Sergey, alas, is unlikely to be aware of the source of his irritation.

Let us imagine another example. This one takes place in an office setting.

> *The energetic, perennially cheerful and merry Valentina (a Leader) suddenly cries out, «Damn the day when I came to this office! I can do nothing here!, I feel as if I am quite incompetent in this work!»*

> *Her superior Anastasia, a very quiet and reserved Structurist, is quite confused. «Look, I never constrain you, never give you orders, and in general try to disturb you as little as possible!»*

> *«That doesn't matter! You can just look at me or put a paper on my desk, and it makes me sick!»*

Valentina's problem is her injured pride. Like any other Leader (I — ●), she attempts to demonstrate to the others that she can manage everything and is perfect in everything. However, logic is a weak function of her type (III — □); being incapable to organize things logically, she masks her vulnerable point with excessive activity and chaotic drive.

Anastasia's ability to act logically and without rush irritates Valentina; she perceives it as a silent reproach of being a bad employee, which is especially painful in view of her high ambitions.

The Leader, in turn, supervises a Psychologist.

In this case, a young woman Catherine (a Psychologist) complains about her mother-in-law Natalie (a Leader):

> *I just cannot hide away from her. Whatever room I enter, whatever I do, there she is with her endless instructions. Even simple shopping is a torture; when I come back, she bothers me with a host of foolish questions: «Where have you been so long?» «Did you stop to chat with somebody?» I just cannot hide away from her. She seems to be ubiquitous!*

Rush and excitement are stressing factors for the Psychologist who has Volitional Sensing in the vulnerable Channel III. Too much activity, too many arguments simply make her nervous. The Leader cannot understand it: in her opinion, she simply takes care, keeps up with events, in other words, does not do anything offending.

Being introverted, a Psychologist periodically needs to stay alone to recover her emotions that accumulate but are kept inside. The Leader's activity is perceived by the Psychologist as attempts to occupy the whole space, to be everywhere, to give orders to everybody and to leave nobody in peace; it is natural that a Psychologist wants to hide away from such obtrusive guardianship.

In turn, the Psychologist supervises a Seeker.

> *Two women, Victoria (Seeker) and Catherine (Psychologist) who were acquainted for many years and always had a lot of interesting ideas to discuss (▲ in Channel I of the Seeker and Channel II of the Psychologist) went together for a week-long business trip and had to stay in the same hotel room. Their relationship began to deteriorate all of a sudden, for no obvious reason but very quickly.*
>
> *It all began as small but unpleasant moments. Victoria liked telling jokes, and one of these jokes she was going to tell in presence of their new acquaintances was, frankly speaking, a little bit spicy. Suddenly she stopped talking and looked at Catherine:*
>
> *I cannot do it. You keep silence, but I see disapproval in your eyes.*

In fact, in this case Victoria simply misunderstood Catherine. The Psychologist, having the Relational Feeling in Channel I, hates conflicts, and in order to avoid them, simply keeps her emotions inside, tries to be calm and tolerant with everybody. On the other hand, the Seeker, having the same function in the vulnerable Channel III, sometimes is not sure of how society perceives her ethically ambiguous actions. Positive emotional reaction can calm the Seeker down, and absence of such reaction is perceived as a reproach. In fact, Catherine did not want to reproach Victoria: she was simply sorry for her friend who behaved so absurdly out of her wrongly understood pride.

> *In another situation, Catherine and Victoria were standing in a long line in the burning sun. Catherine (Psychologist) said to Victoria (Seeker), 'Go sit in the shade; I will stand here alone.»*
>
> *Suddenly Victoria erupted in fury, 'Why do you want to keep me away?»*
>
> *Catherine could not understand the fury—she just wanted to help her friend!*

A Seeker badly understands nuances or intonations; she perceives only logical essence of words and is uncertain of how other people logically evaluate her actions (⌐ – III, Vulnerable Channel). This is why Victoria did not notice the care in the voice of her friend and was offended by understanding Catherine's words as her intention to push Victoria aside.

As we can see, the Psychologist feels offended because she only wanted to help, but her whimsical friend, the Seeker, understands everything conversely. It is probably important for the story that Catherine was much younger; if they were of at least equal age, Victoria would not probably perceive the situation so sharply. Being tired of Catherine's long silence, Victoria felt as if Catherine disapproved of her behavior and wanted to keep her distance under a plausible excuse.

Now can you imagine that people of all these four types work in the same workgroup, worse — in the same room! They will spend all their time quarreling.

This, however, in no way means that people in this room are bad. It is necessary to understand that each individual is not evil by nature. As a rule, people prefer having good relations with other people. However, when a Supervisor and a Supervisee have to interact for a long time, a conflict between them is inevitable. Nonetheless, when communication between partners does not involve the link between the Channels I and III, a conflict may be latent for a long while.

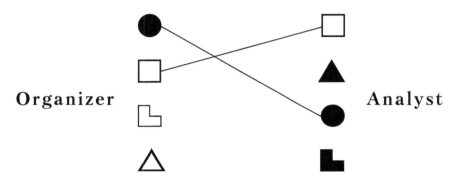

Organizer   **Analyst**

A head of a testing laboratory, Dmitry an Organizer, appointed Nikolay an Analyst, as head of a workgroup. During the several years that followed, while their contact involved only discussion of scientific problems (□ — □ their relationship was stable and professional. When the Soviet Union began to live according to the laws of market economy, the relationship between them began to incorporate a wider range of new issues, such as competing for new contracts and negotiating the payments. The sphere of protecting material interests and competition is relevant to the Volitional Sensing function ●, and discussions related to such issues resulted in a serious conflict. For several months, the working relationships in the laboratory were volcanic, until Nikolay and some of his colleagues finally split and created an independent laboratory.

9. RELATIONSHIP OF IDENTITY

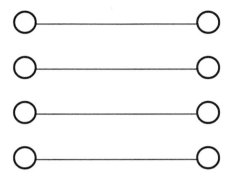

Identity is a relationship between people of the same socionic type. Their informational channels contain identical functions, which means that information is easily transmitted from one of them to the other. This relationship between a teacher and a student is very efficient: nobody else can explain so clearly and teach better than an identical partner. However, as soon as their levels of knowledge become more or less equal, they are no longer interesting to each other because they cannot tell each other anything new. They are both informed about similar matters and respond likewise to similar irritants. They are both strong in the same fields and weak in the same fields, so they cannot expect support of their weak channels from each other and for this reason do not need each other very much. Even discussions gradually become boring because what one of them relates is just a reflection of what the other thinks. If they lived on a desert island, they might lose their ability to speak at all.

However, when a married couple is in a dual relationship and their child inherits one of his parents' types, the child is in a very favorable condition for development. There is no better teacher than your identical partner and no better nurturer than your dual: you always feel support and protection from your dual, she loves you for no obvious reason, just because you are what you are. Unfortunately, in many families only one parent is responsible for nurturing the child. When the nurturing parent is the child's identical partner, the child is provided with good instruction but not with a feeling of security. He does not receive the necessary support for his/her weak functions, has to become self-sufficient, cold-minded, with bottom-line vital attitudes, and with an excessive need for prestige both at work and at home If, however, the child is nurtured only by his dual, then he always feels safe and takes love for granted. However, as adults, such children are very poorly adapted to difficult situations because they have never had to develop their weak functions, which were always protected by their dual parent.

For many children of elementary school age, compatibility with their homeroom or primary teacher may determine their attitude to education for many years to come. When the teacher is of an identical type with the pupil, the latter understands very well what the teacher says, learns easily and earns good credits. Those children whose socionic types are not fully compatible with that of the teacher find studying difficult. Such children can become outsiders, developing complexes and lack of self-confidence.

10. KINDRED RELATIONSHIP

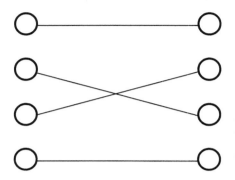

In a kindred relationship, both partners perceive the world similarly in some aspects determined by their common Channel I. In case of cooperation, such relationships may be even fruitful when partners have similar interests and support the weak functions of each other. However, when their interests diverge, the relationship may become unpleasant and annoying, full of small quarrels.

Guardians and Psychologists, both having Relational Feeling in Channel I, are both moralists, holding to high ethical standards. However, interests of Psychologists are always beyond concrete time periods and circumstances. Psychologists, who are also Intuiters, are always thinking about something while walking around. They daydream, project the future, and reflecting on their experiences. In contrast, the thrifty Guardians, being of Sensing types, are focused on everything that takes place around themr: here is a cute cottage at the end of the street, there is a brand new car next door, here is a big tree in bloom on somebody's lot, and there is a man riding a nice bike... Guardians comment on every important detail they notice, and with each of their phrases they bring the Psychologists back from the heaven of their intuitive dreams onto the sinful earth of sensing problems. The Psychologist, being polite, sometimes give brief answers to the Guardians but soon become frustrated and begin to lose his temper, which in turn offends the Guardians.

When they undertake a common business, they can render each other very good assistance, the Psychologists by their capability of foreseeing situations and the Guardians by their capability to take care of the material side.

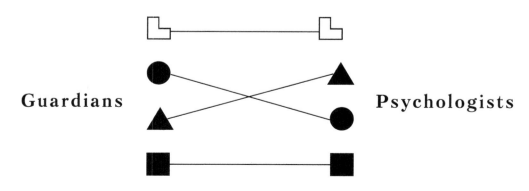

Guardians   Psychologists

11. SUPER-EGO RELATIONSHIP

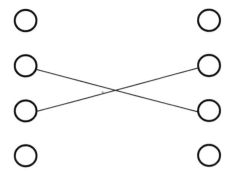

The super-ego relationship is characterized by the same opposition between Channels II and III as the kindred relationship. However, in this case, the problem is aggravated by the difference of functions in the Channel I: interests of the partners are quite different, communication is not easy, and they cannot rely on each other, which often results in disagreements.

While driving, Vladimir, an Enterpreneur, misses a speed limit sign for 25 miles/hour. His wife Alexandra, an Enthusiast, notices it but keeps quiet, being well aware that her husband would not tolerate being reproached (III—○). When the husband sees a police car, he slams on the brakes, and the car skids on the icy road. At that moment, the wife's patience is exhausted, and they begin to quarrel.

Another time, the same couple is going to visit with friends. The wife, afraid of arriving late (III — △), is already completely dressed and waiting at the door, while the husband, still in a bathrobe, asks: «Why are you in such a hurry? We still have a lot of time!» (II — △). Such situations make them quarrel over and over again.

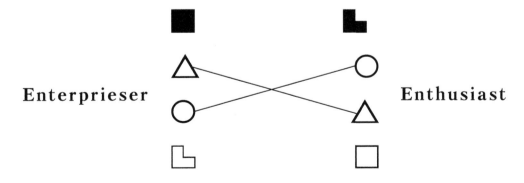

Enterprieser   Enthusiast

12. COLLABORATIVE RELATIONSHIP

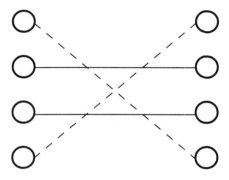

The collaborative relationship is usually calm and stable; having the same function in their strong Channel II, partners understand each other well. When they have common interests, they even can support to a certain extent the partner's Channel IV, although its function is of a different «vertness» than the partner's strong function in his Channel I.

Take the previous example: if the man were not an Enterpreneur but a Professional, he would not have missed the traffic sign. Moreover, since the Professional observes the law with due diligence, he would have slowed down in advance, and the conflict would not have emerged. This couple would not have problems preparing to go out, either, because they both, having △ in the vulnerable Channel III, would have prepared in advance.

13. RELATIONSHIP OF ACTIVATION

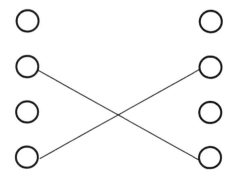

The activation relationship is comfortable although not to such extent as the duality relationship. Each partner's strong («Productive») function of Channel II activates the weak function in Channel IV of the other. This relationship is symmetric; however, it is characterized with a certain amount of tension because of incomplete compensation. Partners can exhaust each other due to the difference of their body rhythms because one of them is rational and the other is labile.

Two friends, Victor and Larissa (whose types are Professional and Initiator) planned to go for a picnic on Sunday. However, a nasty turn in the weather happned. The night right before the trip, it began to rain. The labile Initiator suggested, «Let's go to the movies instead!

The rational Professional was uneasy about changing plans and replied, «What a scatterbrain you are! We have agreed on and are ready for a picnic, and the weather can change for the better.»

This response brought on an exasperated «You bore, can't you forget this trip!» from the Initiator; the impertinence of his friend catches her by surprise.

Such problems usually do not exist in dual pairs because duals are either both rational or both labile.

14. RELATIONSHIP OF QUASI-IDENTITY

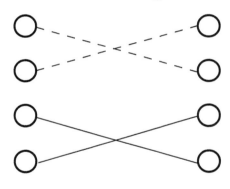

In the quasi-identity relationship the weak functions of the partners are the same but in reverse order. Partners have similar interests because their strong functions are similar even though they are of a different «vertness.» Each one thinks that their partner lacks something really important but for some unknown reason is more successful and competent in many things to which they just do not pay enough attention considering such problems too trivial. The issue here is that communication between their strong channels, I and II, is indirect. As a result, partners may discuss common issues, but use different ways out of difficult situations. Conflicts in this relationship are rare (the Vulnerable Channel is not pressured by any strong function). When the relationship ends, the partners can part easily and without interpersonal friction.

15, 16. RELATIONSHIP OF SOCIAL REQUEST

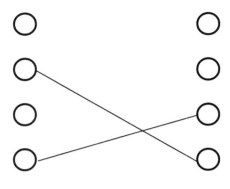

The social-request relationship, similar to the supervision relationship, is asymmetrical. One of the partners is called Transmitter (or Requestor) — from his Productive Channel II he activates the suggestible Channel IV of the Receiver (Requested). This relationship lacks feedback because none of the Receiver's strong functions can influence the Transmitter. This kind of interaction determines the contents of the relationship: everything the Receiver says or does seems to be not very important, redundant to the Transmitter, whereas the latter is perceived by the Receiver as a very important person (due to the function in his Channel II, which produces the request). One cannot ignore this request, because it is accepted by the suggestible Channel IV, which is incapable of critical evaluation of information and thus perceives any request as a must.

Like in the supervision relationship, the social-request relationship makes loops of links between transmitters and receivers. In socionics, such loops are called Social Progress Loops. There are four such loops, in which each of the 16 types is somebody's transmitter and somebody's receiver.

The figure below represents one of these loops. Looking at the above illustration, you will understand how these types request each other, and will be even able to build three other loops.

Table 3.5
An example of a request loop

Channel	Analyst	Craftsman	Guardian	Romantic	Analyst
I, Program	□	○	⌐	△	□
II, Creative	▲	■	●	⌐	▲
III, Vulnerable	●	⌐	▲	■	●
IV, Suggestible	⌐	▲	■	●	⌐

The Transmitter considers the Receiver to be a weaker partner and thus tries to patronize the latter directly or even teach him. Naturally, the Receiver in turn shuns the Transmitter.

Note: *psychological weakness of the Receiver does not necessarily mean his formal subordination to the Transmitter. Quite often we can watch a different picture: a boss (Receiver) and her subordinate (Transmitter) who uses his formally inferior position in order to avoid responsibility for complicated projects, or to make his boss organize things in the way he needs.*

Student Ivan, an Analyst, speaks of his Requestor Constantine, a Romantic:
Arguing with him is useless because he flatly rejects any reasons I give him. It looks like it makes no difference to him whether I say anything or not — he keeps on developing his own idea. I always feel a kind of hidden pressure on me. When I feel like hell while he is in good mood, he tries to get me involved, and I do not like it. When he is looking for any of his belongings, usually a key, he always asks me in such a tone as though it was I who put it away. He never takes seriously my being offended as if he does not realize why I am so angry with him. Just a couple of minutes later he can ask about something quite calmly, with a smile.

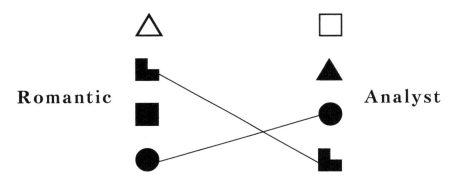

Romantic   **Analyst**

In a family, this relationship may be satisfactory only subject to the Receiver being involved with a lot of activities outside his family, where he can «drain» the energy received from the Transmitter. When he cannot find such diversion, the relationship is most likely to result in a conflict or even break-up.

A group of four types composing a social progress loop can solve various creative tasks very efficiently. Even more efficient is a group of eight types containing two parallel loops. In such a group, all the partners are mobilized, their mental activity is increased, and they do not feel tired for a long time.

Here is an example of such group:

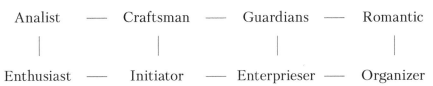

MORE ABOUT
THE RELATIONSHIPS

Strictly speaking, we should have considered not 16 but 1616 = 256 types of relationships, because the nature of each specific relationship depends on the types of partners. For example, in the Psychologist-Guardian kindred pair, both partners seek to establish a warm relationship and are ready to make concessions to obtain it. In contrast, it is impossible to expect mutual concessions in a Leader–Organizer pair because both of these types are competitive by nature, due to their strong Volitional Sensing, and each strives for leadership.

The same peculiarities can be observed in other pairs of types, whatever the relationship may be. This is why it is so important to know the character of each type, its characteristic traits, its strong and weak features, and the relevance of each function to specific situations. For this reason, all you have read in this chapter is a system of coordinates that can be used to predict and understand the nature of the relationship between individuals whose types are known.

Moreover, the nature of relations of real partners strongly depends upon the conditions in which partners interact. For example, duality is a very good relationship for a family because family life requires the manifestation of many different aspects of personality, and duality can provide an optimal complementation between partners. However, in business, duals may be quite dissatisfied with each other. Imagine that a company manager (an Organizer) needs an employee to promote company production on the market. The Organizer's dual, a Romantic, being a compliant, daydreaming, and not very orderly person, will fail in such a position. It would be better to assign the marketing task to an employee who is an Organizer (Appendix I contains good examples of duality and identity relationships between representatives of these two types).

To avoid being misguided by the above descriptions, it is advisable not to take them literally but rather to understand the essence of events and analyze relations from the standpoint of the psyches of the participants.

Above we discussed the backgrounds of intertype relationships as they are considered in Socionics. As you can see, a lot in interpersonal relations is determined by interactions of people's psychological functions, which in Socionics reside in informational channels, because they perceive, process and produce information about different aspects of the world. However, novices in Socionics usually cannot keep in memory all these schemes at once. For this reason, I added a table below that summarizes all the socionic relationships between all the 16 types. You can refer to it, until you understand the principles of Socionics using examples from your own life.

Conventional signs

Quadra: D—duality (complementation), A—activation, I—identity, M—mirror.

Other symmetric relationships: Sd—semi-duality (incomplete complementation), Is—illusion, Kd—kindred, Cb—collaboration, C—contrast, Q—quasi-identity, Se—Super-Ego, Cf—conflict.

Asymmetric relationships: social request: requestor −> receiver; supervision: supervisor +> supervisee.

Table 3.6
Overview of Intertype Relationships (by V. Leshkevichius, 1979)

My partner (columns), myself (rows)	ITE	SFI	FSE	TII	FIE	TSI	STE	IFI	TIE	FSI	SFE	ITI	TSE	FII	IFE	STI
Seeker, ITE	I	D	A	M	->	+>	Cb	Is	Q	Cf	Se	C	<-	<+	Kd	Sd
Epicurean, SFI	D	I	M	A	+>	->	Is	Cb	Cf	Q	C	Se	<+	<-	Sd	Kd
Enthusiast, FSE	A	M	I	D	Kd	Sd	<-	<+	Se	C	Q	Cf	Cb	Is	->	+>
Analyst, TII	M	A	D	I	Sd	Kd	<+	<-	C	Se	Cf	Q	Is	Cb	+>	->
Performer, FIE	<-	<+	Kd	Sd	I	D	A	M	Cb	Is	->	+>	Se	C	Q	Cf
Structurist, TSI	<+	<-	Sd	Kd	D	I	M	A	Is	Cb	+>	->	C	Se	Cf	Q
Organizer, STE	Cb	Is	->	+>	A	M	I	D	<-	<+	Kd	Sd	Q	Cf	Se	C
Romantic, IFI	Is	Cb	+>	->	M	A	D	I	<+	<-	Sd	Kd	Cf	Q	C	Se
Enterpreneur, TIE	Q	Cf	Se	C	Cb	Is	->	+>	I	D	A	M	Kd	Sd	<-	<+
Guardian, FSI	Cf	Q	C	Se	Is	Cb	+>	->	D	I	M	A	Sd	Kd	<+	<-
Leader, SFE	Se	C	Q	Cf	<-	<+	Kd	Sd	A	M	I	D	->	+>	Cb	Is
Critic, ITI	C	Se	Cf	Q	<+	<-	Sd	Kd	M	A	D	I	+>	->	Is	Cb
Professional, TSE	->	+>	Cb	Is	Se	C	Q	Cf	Kd	Sd	<-	<+	I	D	A	M
Psychologist, FII	+>	->	Is	Cb	C	Se	Cf	Q	Sd	Kd	<+	<-	D	I	M	A
Initiator, IFE	Kd	Sd	<-	<+	Q	Cf	Se	C	->	+>	Cb	Is	A	M	I	D
Craftsman, STI	Sd	Kd	<+	<-	Cf	Q	C	Se	+>	->	Is	Cb	M	A	D	I

137

CONCLUDING REMARKS

The readers who have enough patience to get to the end of the book are probably sufficiently interested in this subject to attempt to figure out not only their own psychological types, but also the psychological types of their family, friends, acquaintances, and co-workers.

It is not wrong to suppose that many people will be somewhat disappointed in this aspect: indeed, it all seems so simple and easy in theory, but, in practice, the psychological types are not easy to identify. Thus, the question arises: is it possible that Socionics applies only to very limited number of people who have effortlessly recognizable psychological types, while the majority of us are a «mix» of different types?

Luckily, this is not true, but the question of identifying psychological types turns out to be significantly more complicated than it appeared to be in the early stages of the development of Socionics. It seems that the main difficulty here is the multitude of subtypes under one psychological type. For example, a strengthening of a function in the first or second channel may result in two very different versions of the same psychological type. Thus, on these grounds alone, there are not 16 psychological types, but 32 more subtly differentiated types.

However, this does not cover all of the numerous variants of a basic psychological type. It turns out that there exist many more variants, that 16 types is an intermediate, though very important, stage of dividing people into different psychological types. Rather, we have 16 main groups, in which people have common character traits, but inside each of these groups there are also significant differences that are characteristic to each of the psychological subtypes.

I can predict the disappointment of the reader: «Why did they have to confuse me so much if the division has to be continued? How long does it have to be continued? Won't we end up with a thousand types that can't even be called types anymore, just different people, which will defeat the purpose of this whole typology thing?».

I will try to reply to this frustration, allowing myself the analogy that dividing people into psychological types is like dividing the surface of the earth into oceans, rivers, mountains, and valleys. It is unlikely that any reader will refute the usefulness of general, large-scale maps because they do not have every single little detail on them. Socionics, built on Jung's typology, provides people with a «map» of psychological types, and their relationships. A point can be made that this «map» does not have a very high level of detail yet — however, even now it has a host of practical applications.

Let us discuss in more detail the question of how many subtypes exist in each of the 16 psychological types. The founder of Socionics, Aushra Augustinavichiute, noticed a very interesting fact — a strong physical resemblance between some members of the same psychological type. It seemed to me that this fact was very important, so I began taking photos of the people whose psychological types had been identified reliably enough. Currently, my photo gallery contains about 1500 representatives of different psychological types and can provide us with some very interesting information. In cases where the number of people was large enough (about 150 representatives of the same psychological type), the photographs can be further arranged into smaller groups (more than 10 in each psychological type) in which the faces of the people have a strong resemblance, often no less than the resemblance between twins. The reader has a chance to observe this independently by looking at four pairs out of such smaller groups all belonging to psychological type ITI, or the Critic, shown below.

When these photographs are scrutinized, it comes to mind that nature itself is telling us to take a notice of this phenomenon. People residing as far as 1000 miles away from each other look as if they had strong blood ties. This fact speaks for itself: Jung was able to identify such basic traits that they show up not only psychologically, but physically as well. Often this resemblance also shows up in the tone of voice, in the distinct way people turn their heads, or a specific gait. You get the impression of total physiological and physical similarity. In addition, it turns out that members of the same psychological type are also vulnerable to the same diseases. This tendency is discussed in more detail in the author's book «Personality in the Mirror of Socionics», published in Russia in 2001, where 570 photographs of people of different psychological types are included, as well as almost 100 pairs of «look-alike» portraits.

It is my opinion that the similarity of faces in the subtypes of a psychological type is a reliable reason to believe that we have discovered an «elementary» type, and further differences would have only personal characteristics related to culture, education, family traditions, etc. Currently, it is difficult to assign a certain number to the quantity of subtypes. One thing is certain: within reasonable limits, the number of subtypes in one psychological type is not far above a dozen. It is now essential to find an objective basis for these subdivisions inside a certain type.

In this context, a very promising discovery has been made by Filimonov and Kolchinsky who divided each Jungian functions into two aspects: first related to a person and the second one, to the outside world. For example, Introverted Intuition includes fantasy and imagination as the first aspect, and the sense of time, ability to foresee and predict the course of events as the second aspect. As the result, instead of eight Jungian functions we observe 16 aspects, and each psychological type naturally divides into four

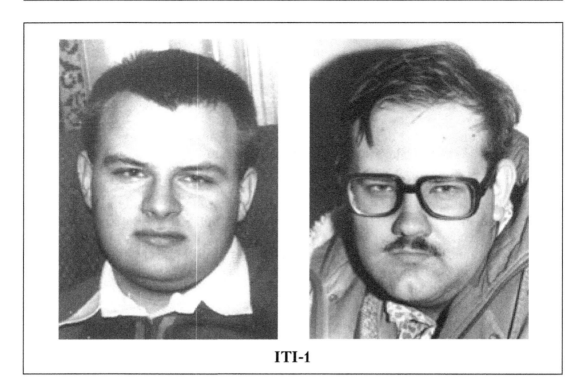

ITI-1

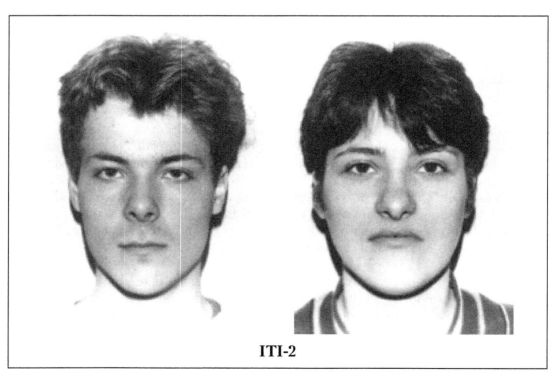

ITI-2

ITI-3

ITI-4

subtypes. Considering the above mentioned possibility of strengthening the function in the first or the second channel, each psychological type falls into eight distinctively different subtypes.

It is possible that the solution to the problem of the complete classification of types and subtypes will be found in a physiological approach, in defining a set of discrete parameters that vary for different people, but stay unchanged though the lifetime, like, for example, the blood type. Important information can probably be received, studying the asymmetry of human brain, and, correspondingly, its outer manifestations resulting in the asymmetry of the face, use of left and right hands, etc. There is also some research regarding which of the various sensory systems (visual, auditory, and kinesthetic) the psychological types prefer to use — this field also requires additional studies. All these data could help to solve the most essential problem in Socionics (as well as any other typology) — the reliability of identification of individual psychological type.

So what are the problems that Socionics can help to solve today?

First of all consider the problem of determination of psychological traits and strong and weak points of a person, and their professional orientation. Enough time was devoted to this question in the main text of this book.

It is probably unnecessary to explain in detail how important the knowledge of socionic laws of compatibility is to couples who are planning to get married and start a family. Extra caution must be exhibited in the cases where two people who are not compatible from the viewpoint of Socionics cannot (and, more importantly, should not) live apart from each other. Ailing family members, elderly parents, and problem children fit into this category. Moral issues become the first priority, and therefore, Socionics can help the individuals reasonably acknowledge all the difficulties of a their life together, develop strategy and tactics for socializing, and, in particular, realize that they cannot blame each other in the situations where the behavior is dictated by the differences in their psychological types. In these situations, it is necessary, when possible, to limit the communication of the «conflicting» channels. To run away, leave, or ignore are, of course, very tempting and simple alternatives. It sometimes happens that there is simply no other choice. However, in any case, the main foundation for such decisions must be provided by ethical and moral principles.

One of the most perspective applications of Socionics is in the formation of so-called «small groups» of three or four people working together on a common project. This is probably the best practical use of Socionics. These groups may be research groups in a laboratory, work shifts, geological parties, space teams, or polar expeditions. This list also includes groups of sick people who can therapeutically influence each other, students who find that they are assigned to live at the same dorm room in college, and also friends or colleagues who decide to share a vacation home. In conclusion, I would like to discuss one more particularly important aspect. Classic psychoanalysis is based on the personal history of an individual, on the psychological worries that the person experienced in childhood, which may have a serious effect on the rest of the person's life. Due to this, the job of a psychoanalyst consists in locating and excavating the core of such negative worries, destroying their energy, and, in this way, helping individuals to become better suited to their own lives.

On the other hand, Socionics, studies the inborn traits of personality, which remain unchanged throughout the entire lifetime of the individual. Although some characteristic qualities are refined and strengthened, allowing a person to better adapt to the constantly changing environment, these refinements do not alter the foundation of the psychological type. This view is justified by a phenomenal physical similarity between members of the same «elementary» psychological subtype that often astounds people. Only genetic determination of a psychological type could explain its stability throughout the lifetime of a person and explain the phenomenon of «socionic twins», doppelgangers, or look-alikes.

On that I will have to say good bye to you, my dear Reader. I sincerely hope that what you have read in this book has helped you to solve some of psychological problems that all of us encounter in our everyday lives. I wish you good luck and plenty of happiness.

Appendix I

Analysis of Psychological Peculiarities of the Heroes of M.Mitchell's gone with the wind and their relations from the Socionic Standpoint

My impression of reading many literary works is that many writers, especially those whose names became famous, felt intuitively psychological constitution of their heroes and described them so exactly as though they were familiar with Socionics.

In this Appendix we propose our reader to recall the heroes of M.Mitchell's Gone with the Wind (Scarlett, Ellen, Rhett Butler, Ashley Wilkes and Melanie) and to analyze both their psychological types and their relations from the standpoint of Socionics.

The events of the novel Gone with the Wind take place in the mid of the XIX century during the civil war between the North and the South. Scarlett is a daughter of a farmer Gerald O'Hara and his wife Ellen, and they are Southerners.

Here is how the 16-years-old Scarlett expresses her principles to her Black nurse Mammy, when the last tries to teach Scarlett right, from her standpoint, behavior:

> I'm tired of everlastingly being unnatural and never doing anything I want to do. I'm tired of acting like I don't eat more than a bird, and walking when I want to run and saying I feel faint after a waltz, when I could dance for two days and never get tired. I'm tired of saying, 'How wonderful you are!' to fool men who haven't got one-half the sense I've got, and I'm tired of pretending I don't know anything, so men can tell me things and feel important while they're doing it...

Even this small fragment is a valid evidence of Scarlett's being a Thinking type. She does not care much for acceptable norms of social behavior and calls things by their proper plain names.

Scarlett attracts a lot of young men in her neighborhood, but she loves Ashley Wilkes whom she has known from her bottle up. She believes Ashley loves her too, and her vanity is much injured by news about Ashley's engagement with her cousin Melanie.

When she finds a moment to stay alone with Ashley, she explains herself according to her principles:

> *Why don't you say it, you coward! You're afraid to marry me! You'd rather live with that stupid little fool who can't open her mouth except to say 'Yes' or 'No' and raise a passel of mealy-mouthed brats just like her! Why—*
>
> *You must not say these things about Melanie!*
>
> *'I mustn't' be damned to you! Who are you to tell me I mustn't? You coward, you cad, you— You made me believe you were going to marry me—*
>
> *«Be fair,» his voice pleaded. «Did I ever—»*
>
> *She did not want to be fair, although she knew what he said was true. He had never once crossed the borders of friendliness with her and, when she thought of this fresh anger rose, the anger of hurt pride and feminine vanity (...)*
>
> *She sprang to her feet, her hands clenched and he rose towering over her, his face full of the mute misery of one forced to face realities when realities are agonies (...)*
>
> *«Scarlett—please—»*
>
> *He put out his hand toward her and, as he did, she slapped him across the face with all the strength she had. The noise cracked like a whip in the still room and suddenly her rage was gone, and there was desolation in her heart (...).*
>
> *Her hand dropped to a little table beside her, fingering a tiny china rose-bowl on which two china cherubs smirked. The room was so still she almost screamed to break the silence. She must do something or go mad. She picked up the bowl and hurled it viciously across the room toward the fireplace. It barely cleared the tall back of the sofa and splintered with a little crash against the marble mantelpiece.*

The reader will definitely agree that Scarlett is characterized first and foremost by volitional pressure and decisiveness. She wants to achieve her goals at any costs and makes no bones about the means. Scarlett's whole behavior is very characteristic for the pragmatic type Sensing-Thinking Extravert, which is called The Organizer in Socionics.

The world in the eyes of The Organizer is a battlefield where different forces collide; it is always necessary to monitor these forces and to calculate their direction. Like nobody else, The Organizer is capable of estimating the essence of a here-and-now situation. This type's consciousness is not hindered by ethical restrictions, it is concrete, and lability allows reacting promptly to all changes in the current situation.

Here is a characteristic example of Scarlett's behavior:

> *A Yankee, a Yankee with a long pistol on his hip! And she was alone in the house with three sick girls and the babies!!*

As he lounged up the walk, hand on holster, beady little eyes glancing to right and left, a kaleidoscope of jumbled pictures spun in her mind, stories Aunt Pittypat had whispered of attacks on unprotected women, throat cuttings, houses burned over the heads of dying women, children bayoneted because they cried, all of the unspeakable horrors that lay bound up in the name of «Yankee.» (...)

She slipped off her worn shoe and, barefooted, she pattered swiftly to the bureau, not even feeling her festered toe. She opened the top drawer soundlessly and caught up the heavy pistol she had brought from Atlanta. (...) She fumbled in the leather box that hung on the wall below his saber and brought out a cap. She slipped it into place with a hand that did not shake. Quickly and noiselessly, she ran into the upper hall and down the stairs, steadying herself on the banisters with one hand and holding the pistol close to her thigh in the folds of her skirt(...).

... She could only stare over the banisters at him and watch his face change from harsh tenseness to a half-contemptuous, half-ingratiating smile.

«So there is somebody ter home,» he said, slipping his pistol back into its holster and moving into the hall until he stood directly below her. «All alone, little lady?»

Like lightning, she shoved her weapon over the banisters and into the startled bearded face. Before he could even fumble at his belt, she pulled the trigger. The back kick of the pistol made her reel, as the roar of the explosion filled her ears and the acrid smoke stung her nostrils. The man crashed backwards to the floor, sprawling into the dining room (...)

Yes, he was dead. Undoubtedly. She had killed a man.

This is how quickly and exactly this young girl estimated how dangerous the situation was for her and for all those weak and defenseless who were in the house. Without any shade of doubt and hesitation she immediately made a decision and fulfilled it. It is very probable that she chose the only possible way out of the situation that represented a serious danger for her and everybody around her.

It is easier for that type to give effectual help than to weep tears of compassion. Our heroine, Scarlett, was in a difficult situation: Melanie, the wife of Ashley so much beloved to her Ashley was about to give birth to a child, but she could not expect for outside help when Yankees approached the city and everybody left it. They had to go too, but Scarlett could not leave Melanie in danger.

«They're coming,» whispered Melanie undeceived and buried her face in the pillow. (...) Oh, Scarlett, you mustn't stay here. You must go and take Wade.»

What Melanie said was no more than Scarlett had been thinking but hearing it put into words infuriated her, shamed her as if her secret cowardice was written plainly in her face.

> *«Don't be a goose. I'm not afraid. You know I won't leave you.»*
>
> *«You might as well. I'm going to die.» And she began moaning again (...)*
>
> *It was all over. Melanie was not dead and the small baby boy who made noises like a young kitten was receiving his first bath at Prissy's hands.*

Such, say the least of it, indelicate manners are characteristic for many sensing-thinking extraverts (The Organizer) in complicated situations. This is a particular example of the Relational Feeling function in the (vulnerable) Channel III of this type — Heaven forbid anybody to suspect him/her of being spineless and maudlin! Even women of this psychological type shrink from manifesting tender feelings, sometimes it may look as though they do not need such feelings at all. The truth, however, is different. They have various feelings just like other people do, however, they perceive these feelings as manifestation of weakness which they are afraid to demonstrate and reluctant to complain about.

Regarding the sphere of mystery, vague premonitions, unclear daydreams (Temporal Intuition, Channel IV), The Organizer sometimes realizes he is devoid of this side in his life and feels deep appreciation to those who can reveal him this unexplored world and to enrich his soul. It is Ashley's lyricism and mystique, love for music and delicacy of his nature that attract Scarlett to him so much; he is dowered with exactly those aspects of personality that Scarlett lacks so desperately.

One more hero of the same Margaret Mitchell's novel belongs to the same type, The Organizer—this of course is Rhett Butler. Here are some quotes from the novel that testify in favor of such evaluation of his nature:

> *He was a tall man and powerfully built. Scarlett thought she had never seen a man with such wide shoulders, so heavy with muscles, almost too heavy for gentility. When her eye caught his, he smiled, showing animal-white teeth below a close-clipped black mustache. He was dark of face, swarthy as a pirate, and his eyes were as bold and black as any pirate's appraising a galleon to be scuttled or a maiden to be ravished. There was a cool recklessness in his face and a cynical humor in his mouth as he smiled at her, and Scarlett caught her breath.*

This fragment is a very good description of Rhett's Volitional Sensing; he is a person ready to conquer everything he sees and to rule.

When all people are full of patriotic enthusiasm and are ready to stand for their values, Rhett disregards public opinion and expresses absolutely contrary opinion about the situation of the Confederacy, which is later proved by events of the war. Rhett is very flexible, he is brilliant in using all opportunities, calculating all his moves, and without any scruple makes pile out of that war:

> *«And the Yankees help me make my money. Why, last month I sailed my boat right into New York harbor and took on a cargo.»*
>
> *«What!» cried Scarlett, interested and excited in spite of herself. «Didn't they shell you?»*

*«My poor innocent! Of course not. There are plenty of sturdy Union patri-
ots who are not averse to picking up money selling goods to the Confederacy. I run my boat into New York, buy from Yankee firms, sub rosa, of
course, and away I go. And when that gets a bit dangerous, I go to Nas-
sau where these same Union patriots have brought powder and shells and
hoop skirts for me. It's more convenient than going to England. Sometimes
it's a bit difficult running it into Charleston or Wilmington—but you'd be
surprised how far a little gold goes.» (...).They know the Confederacy will
be licked eventually, so why shouldn't they cash in on it?*

Rhett prefers to call things by their proper names and does not much care for bon
ton of his statements—just like Scarlett does herself:

*Rhett said frankly that the crepe veil made her look like a crow and the
black dresses added ten years to her age.*

Scarlett's and Rhett Butler's socionic types having been determined correctly, we
see a pair of identical types.

Identity, as it follows from the term, is a relationship between partners belonging
to the same type. In this case we can expect complete understanding of motivation of
all actions and expressions of each other, since all the channels are filled with the same
functions.

Partners sometimes do not like such understanding—such mutual transparency,
after all, infringes one's privacy. Let us recall how Rhett Butler understands all Scarlett's hidden thoughts at once, which sometimes even fears her.

Channel	Rhett, The Organizer	Scarlett, The Organizer
I, Program	●————————●	
II, Creative	□————————□	
III, Vulnerable	⌐————————⌐	
IV, Suggestible	△————————△	

*Again he had made a graceful remark, the kind of compliment any
gentleman would pay under such circumstances, but he did not mean
a word of it. He was jeering at her. He knew she hadn't loved Charles.
And Melly was just a big enough fool not to see through him. Oh, please
God, don't let anybody else see through him, she thought with a start of*

terror. Would he tell what he knew? (...).She looked up at him and saw that his mouth was pulled down at the corners in mock sympathy, even while he swished the fan. (...).

«Fear not, fair lady! Your guilty secret is safe with me!»

«Oh,» she whispered, feverishly, «how can you say such things!»

«I only thought to ease your mind» (...)

She met his eyes unwillingly and saw they were as teasing as a small boy's. Suddenly she laughed.

However, we need to repeat once again that Socionics considers psychological types *ceteris paribus* (i.e. as though all other conditions are equal or negligible). Scarlett and Rhett, representing the same socionic type, are nevertheless not completely identical personalities. First of all, they are different by their sex; secondly, they belong to different subtypes; finally, Rhett is much older than Scarlett, and this is why she so often adopts his thought on such matters where she is not much competent and has not yet formed her slant.

Author's note: often psychological difference between people of the same type is determined by amplification of one of the leading channels, I or II. In this case, Scarlett's subtype and her behavior are determined more by the Volitional Sensing and less by Thinking. Rhett Butler's behavior is, by contrast, more determined by Thinking. I consider the issue of subtypes to be very important, but have to skip this problem in my book because of its limited volume.

> *Her audience was speechless with horror.*
>
> *«I'm tired of sitting at home and I'm not going to do it any longer. If they all talked about me about last night, then my reputation is already gone and it won't matter what else they say.»*
>
> *It did not occur to her that the idea was Rhett Butler's. It came so patly and fitted so well with what she was thinking.*

The character of their matrimonial relationship is one more valid proof of their belonging to the type The Organizer. Being born conquerors (like all other Organizers with Volitional Sensing in the Channel I), both spouses always try to prove their superiority, and none of them is ready to concede. Finally they have to part, because marriage is impossible without compromise solutions and readiness to concede at least on the part of one of the partners.

Strictly speaking, identical relationships are different for each specific couple. While the pair of two Organizers (sensing-thinking extraverts) is unlikely to be happy in marriage, like Scarlett and Rhett, two Epicureans (sensing-feeling introverts) with their usual strive to avoid conflicts and to make mutual concessions, or two Guardians (feeling-sensing introverts), strictly adherent to moral norms, may be happy together. The author considers this issue in details in her book Socionics of Personal Attitudes published in 2005 in Russian (Moscow, Dobroye Slovo Publishers).

Now we are going to consider psychological characteristics of Ellen, Scarlett's mother. In all her deeds she is attached to the leading idea of moral, rules of human communication, necessity of keeping certain approvable lifestyle. Her behavior is very descriptive for the type The Guardian (feeling-sensing introvert).

Let us recall characteristic episodes of Ellen's behavior. When she happens to learn that Scarlett participated in a charitable party in mourning after the death of her husband, she writes a letter to her daughter:

> *It is difficult for me to believe that you could so forget yourself and your rearing. I will pass over the impropriety of your appearing publicly while in mourning, realizing your warm desire to be of assistance to the hospital. But to dance, and with such a man as Captain Butler! I have heard much of him (as who has not?) and Pauline wrote me only last week that he is a man of bad repute and not even received by his own family in Charleston, except of course by his heartbroken mother. He is a thoroughly bad character who would take advantage of your youth and innocence to make you conspicuous and publicly disgrace you and your family (...).*

> *«I am heartbroken to think that you could so soon forget your rearing. I have thought of calling you home immediately but will leave that to your father's discretion. He will be in Atlanta Friday to speak with Captain Butler and to escort you home.»*

At first meeting, this type exhibits delicacy, tact and compliance; however, sooner or later, The Guardian reveals volitional features of his/her nature, especially when implementation of his/her vital principles meets obstacles. In the last case he/she acts with decision and insistence.

> *There was a steely quality under her stately gentleness that awed the whole household, Gerald as well as the girls, though he would have died rather than admit it. (...). Mother had always been just as she was, a pillar of strength, a fount of wisdom, the one person who knew the answers to everything.*

The Guardian is strong in managing everyday chores, he is thrifty and assiduous.

> *From the day when Ellen first came to Tara, the place had been transformed. If she was only fifteen years old, she was nevertheless ready for the responsibilities of the mistress of a plantation. (...) She quickly brought order, dignity and grace into Gerald's household, and she gave Tara a beauty it had never had before (...)*

> *She became the best-loved neighbor in the County. She was a thrifty and kind mistress, a good mother and a devoted wife. The heartbreak and selflessness that she would have dedicated to the Church were devoted instead to the service of her child, her household and the man who had taken her out of Savannah and its memories and had never asked any questions.*

From this fragment we notice once again Ellen's traditionalism; she keeps fidelity to stable principles that make foundations of all her life, as The Guardian usually does.

And finally, here is one more fragment from the novel containing the essence of Ellen's nature:

> *Ellen's life was not easy, nor was it happy, but she did not expect life to be easy, and, if it was not happy, that was woman's lot. It was a man's world, and she accepted it as such. The man owned the property, and the woman managed it. The man took the credit for the management, and the woman praised his cleverness. The man roared like a bull when a splinter was in his finger, and the woman muffled the moans of childbirth, lest she disturb him. Men were rough of speech and often drunk. Women ignored the lapses of speech and put the drunkards to bed without bitter words. Men were rude and outspoken, women were always kind, gracious and forgiving.*

Her husband Gerald is a blustery and seemingly rude person (which is just a surface impression—he just does not like to disclose his feelings). And Ellen is both soft enough to calm down his temperament and strong enough to spend the whole night sitting at an old black woman's bed and to help her deliver a child.

> *Gerald's face had brightened as if by magic at her entrance.*
>
> *«Is the brat baptized?» he questioned.*
>
> *«Yes, and dead, poor thing,» said Ellen. «I feared Emmie would die too, but I think she will live.»*
>
> *The girls' faces turned to her, startled and questioning, and Gerald wagged his head philosophically.*
>
> *«Well, 'tis better so that the brat is dead, no doubt, poor fatherle—»*
>
> *It is late. We had better have prayers now,» interrupted Ellen so smoothly that, if Scarlett had not known her mother well, the interruption would have passed unnoticed.*

Let us notice that typical Guardians are tactful, avoid unnecessary conflicts, which we can see from the above fragment. Characters of spouses complement each other well, this is why

> *Gerald's face had brightened as if by magic at her entrance.*

Let us consider now Scarlett's relation with her mother. We need to notice that the partners are not in equal positions, since we talk about a mother and a daughter — and socionic relationships are best visible when all other conditions are equal. From the tender nail Scarlett used to learn the norms of behavior from her mother. This role in Socionics is played by the function of Relational Feeling which occupies the mother's Channel I and the daughter's Channel III. Being theoretically painful from the standpoint of Socionics, such kind of teaching is, on the other hand, quite a normal function of any mother towards her daughter.

Channel	Ellen, The Guardian	Scarlett, The Organizer
I, Program		
II, Creative		
III, Vulnerable		
IV, Suggestible		

This relationship is the mother's supervision of her daughter.

Each of us often admires such psychological traits of other people that he lacks himself, and this is what we see in this case. Scarlett sincerely tries to be polite like her mother but always fails and is unlikely to succeed. Knowing her nature, we cannot even imagine anyone else who can afford making such moral teaching to Scarlett—her harsh reaction follows immediately.

Let us consider now Ashley Wilkes whom Scarlett loves so much and who was so expressively portrayed in the novel:

> *And now, for the first time in her life, she was facing a complex nature.*

> *For Ashley was born of a line of men who used their leisure for thinking, not doing, for spinning brightly colored dreams that had in them no touch of reality. He moved in an inner world that was more beautiful than Georgia and came back to reality with reluctance. He looked on people, and he neither liked nor disliked them. He looked on life and was neither heartened nor saddened. He accepted the universe and his place in it for what they were and, shrugging, turned to his music and books and his better world.*

Ashley is one of those few who understand how senseless that war was, who realize all its essence and foresaw the ignominious end of the Confederate Army. All these thoughts make him feel depressed and he shares his apprehension with his wife Melanie:

> *I am not afraid of danger or capture or wounds or even death, if death must come, but I do fear that once this war is over, we will never get back to the old times. And I belong in those old times. I do not belong in this mad present of killing and I fear I will not fit into any future, try though I may. Nor will you, my dear, for you and I are of the same blood. I do not know what the future will bring, but it cannot be as beautiful or as satisfying as the past. (...)*

I should not write those words. I should not even think them. But you have asked me what was in my heart, and the fear of defeat is there (...). We should have paid heed to cynics like Butler who knew, instead of statesmen who felt—and talked.

From all the above we see an intuitive type, most probably a Romantic (intuitive-feeling introvert). We know that people of this type are capable of anticipating imminent events, feeling even slightest vibes of community spirit and its dynamics. Like other people of this type, Ashley feels very exactly when it is time to act, apprehends dangers and crisis situations.

People of this psychological type like reading fiction, novels; in their daydreams they participate in all the adventures and romances of fictional heroes.

The Romantic is The Organizer's dual; this is probably why Scarlett finds in him what she lacks and loves him so much.

Channel	Ashley, The Romantic	Scarlett, The Organizer
I, Program	△	●
II, Creative	◢	□
III, Vulnerable	■	⌐
IV, Suggestible	●	△

Finally, let us try to understand the type of Melanie, Ashley's wife and Scarlett's «rival», as well as relationships in this married couple.

The following fragment from the novel is very descriptive to Melanie's nature:

...she always saw the best in everyone and remarked kindly upon it. There was no servant so stupid that she did not find some redeeming trait of loyalty and kind-heartedness, no girl so ugly and disagreeable that she could not discover grace of form or nobility of character in her, and no man so worthless or so boring that she did not view him in the light of his possibilities rather than his actualities.

From this fragment we notice one of the most characteristic features of The Psychologist (feeling-intuitive introvert)—the strive to remark in each person first of all his or her positive traits. However, this quality is pertinent to some other types as well; there are some more moments in Melanie's behavior and motivation that allow considering her as a Psychologist.

In particular, Melanie was known for her strong sense of duty. This is why Melanie became so furious when Scarlett just supposed that Ashley could take an oath to the enemy to save his life:

> *«Why didn't he take the oath and then desert and come home as soon as he got out of jail?»*
>
> *Melanie turned on her like a small fury.*
>
> *«How can you even suggest that he would do such a thing? Betray his own Confederacy by taking that vile oath and then betray his word to the Yankees! I would rather know he was dead at Rock Island than hear he had taken that oath. I'd be proud of him if he died in prison. But if he did THAT, I would never look on his face again. Never! Of course, he refused.»*

Melanie is not afraid of advocating Rhett Butler whose realistic evaluation of the situation makes patriotic Southerners indignant. In this case Melanie is ready to fight up to the last ditch, although usually a Psychologist is a very peaceful person and very hardly bears such conflicting situations:

> *Melanie's hands were shaking but she went on hurriedly, as though fearing her courage would fail her if she delayed*
>
> *«I won't be rude to him because of what he said, because — It was rude of him to say it out loud — most ill advised — but it's — it's what Ashley thinks. And I can't forbid the house to a man who thinks what my husband thinks. It would be unjust.»*
>
> *Mrs. Merriwether's breath had come back and she charged.*
>
> *«Melly Hamilton, I never heard such a lie in all my life! There was never a Wilkes who was a coward —»*
>
> *«I never said Ashley was a coward,» said Melanie, her eyes beginning to flash. «I said he thinks what Captain Butler thinks, only he expresses it in different words. And he doesn't go around saying it at musicales, I hope. But he has written it to me.»*

One more important remark. The Psychologist's sensing function is very weak. Health care issues do not belong to this type's inborn expertise and quickly make him/her exhausted—and Melanie works in a hospital and helps wounded soldiers. However, even in such situations Melanie's sense of duty helps her. She is disgusted by seeing septic wounds, truncated bodies, but she never shows how hard it is for her to see all these things:

> *Melanie, however, did not seem to mind the smells, the wounds or the nakedness, which Scarlett thought strange in one who was the most timorous and modest of women. Sometimes when holding basins and instruments while Dr. Meade cut out gangrened flesh, Melanie looked very*

white. And once, alter such an operation, Scarlett found her in the linen closet vomiting quietly into a towel. But as long as she was where the wounded could see her, she was gentle, sympathetic and cheerful, and the men in the hospitals called her an angel of mercy.

What kind of relationship exists between Melanie and Ashley?

They both belong to the same socionic group of occupational mindsets (Humanist, intuitive + feeling), this is why they have common interests and are alike in many aspects. However, one important thing is different: one of them is a rational type and another is labile, therefore their synonymic strong functions, Intuition and Feeling, have different «vertness» and stand in reverse order.

Channel	Ashley, The Romantic	Melanie, The Psychologist
I, Program	△	⊐
II, Creative	◣	▲
III, Vulnerable	■	●
IV, Suggestible	●	■

Here is what Ashley tells about Melanie:

«She is like me, part of my blood, and we understand each other. Scarlett! Scarlett! Can't I make you see that a marriage can't go on in any sort of peace unless the two people are alike?»

Some one else had said that: «Like must marry like or there'll be no happiness.»

Knowing Socionics, we can only partly agree with Ashley. He and Scarlett are duals, this is why Scarlett was intuitively inclined to him. However, after all, Scarlett married Rhett Butler, a man of the same type as she, but their marriage finally failed and the happy end proposed by Alexandra Ripley in her sequel novel Scarlett is not psychologically justified.

Melanie and Ashley are happy together, but let us not forget that they both belong to the well-offs and very often can afford relying on slaves in practical issues (i.e. relevant to thinking and sensing, their weakest functions). On the other hand, no wonder that Ashley, going up the line, asks his dual Scarlett to take care about Melanie in the hard war time. And in fact Scarlett, with her outstanding durability so characteristic to the Organizer type, later saves Melanie and her newborn child, Ashley's son. Ashley could scarcely do it as good as Scarlett did.

Let us notice that duals very often take no notice of each other, because their two leading functions are different, and they cannot find common interests through initial superficial contacts. This is what Ashley means when he unsuccessfully persuades Scarlett to abandon him. By contrast, Scarlett, being a born conqueror, cannot forget him, especially because she is socionically right. Once again we need to notice that even in symmetrical socionic relationships each types behaves in his/her own way, depending on his/her inborn traits.

Finally, let us analyze the relationship between Scarlett and Melanie who belong to the types Organizer and Psychologist:

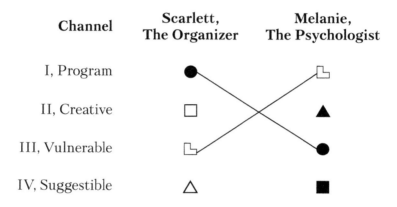

Channel	Scarlett, The Organizer	Melanie, The Psychologist
I, Program	●	⌐
II, Creative	□	▲
III, Vulnerable	⌐	●
IV, Suggestible	△	■

One can mention that their relationship in the novel is aggravated by jealousy— Scarlett loves Ashley who marries Melanie. Isn't it Scarlett's subjective attitude towards Melanie that she is so scornful about her «ugliness», her fragility, her almost childish weakness and helplessness. It is true that sensing types, compared to intuitive, often look stronger, more shapely, physically sound. In this regard Scarlett, being a sensing-thinking extravert, obviously gets the bulge on the feeling-intuitive Melanie, and the last can even sometimes feel inferior in comparison with Scarlett.

However, when the question is about spiritual tenacity, the weak and subtle Melanie leads, and Scarlett has nothing as to accept her leadership. Let us remind the fragment where Melanie opposes the public opinion about Rhett Butler:

Melanie was white and her eyes were enormous.

> *«I will speak to him again,» she said in a low voice. «I will not be rude to him. I will not forbid him the house.»(...)*

> *«Now, why didn't I have the gumption to say that?» thought Scarlett, jealousy mixing with admiration. «How did that little rabbit ever get up spunk enough to stand up to old lady Merriwether?»*

Well, the reader may say, since we believe that Rhett Butler belongs to the same type as Scarlett, why is his relationship to Melanie «conflicting»? The novel shows quite a different picture: Rhett holds Melanie in respect and even supports her. For example, during charitable fundraising for army Melanie sacrifices her wedding ring, her memory about Ashley and her link with him, for the good of the common struggle. Rhett ransoms the ring and gives it back to Melanie:

> *«I was crying because I'm so happy,» and suddenly she opened her clenched palm and pressed some object that was in it to her lips. «I'm so happy,» and burst into tears again.*
>
> *Scarlett caught a fleeting glimpse and saw that it was a broad gold ring.*
>
> *«Read it,» said Melly, pointing to the letter on the floor. «Oh, how sweet, how kind, he is!»*
>
> *Scarlett, bewildered, picked up the single sheet and saw written in a black, bold hand: «The Confederacy may need the lifeblood of its men but not yet does it demand the heart's blood of its women. Accept, dear Madam, this token of my reverence for your courage and do not think that your sacrifice has been in vain, for this ring has been redeemed at ten times its value. Captain Rhett Butler.»*

Margaret Mitchell, the novel author, was quite right in this case. Why does Rhett care so much for Melanie then? And why is this relationship called conflicting? The reasons why Scarlett dislikes Melanie are obvious, but does Rhett treat her so differently?

This seeming contradiction is easy to explain. A conflicter may attract from the far distance, even awake admiration, because he/she possesses such traits which are unachievable for his/her partner. Moreover, what people admire in their conflicters belong to their most painful and vulnerable weaknesses. And Rhett Butler's attitude towards Melanie is just the case. Being a pragmatic person up to cynicism, he respects Melanie's spirituality, her fidelity to her ideals of abstract humanism and ability to stand for these ideals.

> *«If I am 'nicer' to Mrs. Wilkes, it is because she deserves it. She is one of the very few kind, sincere and unselfish persons I have ever known. But perhaps you have failed to note these qualities. And moreover, for all her youth, she is one of the few great ladies I have ever been privileged to know», tells Rhett about Melanie.*

In the same way, in spite of the negative public opinion, Melanie behaves towards Rhett Butler. She defends him from accusations and gossips, since he is capable of making pragmatic deeds so unusual for Melanie herself, because all these deeds require strong sensing and thinking. Rhett's strong and Melanie's weak functions:

I think people are acting like chickens with their heads off about Captain Butler. I'm sure he can't be all the bad things Dr. Meade and Mrs. Merriwether say he is. He wouldn't hold food from starving people. Why, he even gave me a hundred dollars for the orphans. I'm sure he's just as loyal and patriotic as any of us and he's just too proud to defend himself. You know how obstinate men are when they get their backs up.»

Time after time each of us could observe good and supporting relations between people belonging to conflicting types. With one but important remark: such relations are always kept at a long distance. Once partners come into closer contact, or even worse—get married, conflicts and disagreements are inevitable and often result in divorces.

My book Personality's Reflection in the Mirror of Socionics (published in Russian in 2000) includes, in addition to a lot of pictures of people belonging to different types, many examples of all the 16 socionic types from the works of Leo Tolstoy, Fyodor Dostoyevsky, Alexander Dumas, Margaret Mitchell, Erich Maria Remarque and many other authors.

Appendix II

Dichotomy test to determine sychological types (developed by the author of the book)

Offering this questionnaire to the readers, I am well aware that no test is perfect and even answering all of the questions does not guarantee correct determination of one's own psychological type, more so those of the other people. Nevertheless, personality tests give them valuable information about themselves.

From my experience of many years in Socionics I am convinced that 100% reliable tests or questionnaires have not been yet created, nor am I sure that such tests are possible in principle. When determining the type, one should rely not only and not as much on the test result as on many other factors, such as mimics, gestures, gait, appearance, tone of the voice, characteristics of speech, and many others. This is why I ask my readers to be cautious with the interpretation of the test results.

> *(Translator's note: there may be also intercultural shifts in answering test questions: people of one nation, depending on their culture, tend to increase or decrease their scores on some questions; due to local traditions, the average score of all participants' answers to the question I.1 of the below test is expected to be lower in the Western Europe and higher in South Korea. Another example: Anglo-Saxon or German people tend to answer «yes» to the question III.2, while to people of Russia or Spain this choice is less socially important).*

First, draw a table of 4 lines and XII columns. The questions are grouped by 4. Fill in the columns by answering them one by one.

I	II	III	IV	V	VI	VII	VIII	IX	X	XI	XII

Each question contains two options, a) and b) respectively. Depending on your choice, you will need to put one of the following figures in a respective cell: 1, 3, 5, 7, 9:

Usually a) – 1;

Rather a) than b) – 3;

I cannot make a choice – 5;

Rather b) than a) – 7;

Usually b) – 9.

The column XI serves to add up the totals for columns I-X in each of the lines, and the column XII to enter the interpretation of numerical results using the key below.

I

1. If I need a little help,

a) I would easily approach people whom I do not know well (1, 3),

b) I would rather sustain some discomfort than ask other people (7, 9).

2. When doing something,

a) I find it difficult to switch to a different task, necessity to do so frustrates me (1,3),

b) I can easily multitask, such situations are normal for me (7, 9).

3. If I receive unpleasant news,

a) It makes my sleep uneasy (1, 3),

b) My sleep rarely depends on my daily troubles (7, 9).

4. Uncertainty about my distant future

a) Does not concern me: unexpected things happen all the time, and one cannot be prepared for everything (1, 3),

b) Worries me: I easily imagine a lot of problems that may happen one day (7, 9).

II

1. When I do not like the situation,

a) I will not tolerate it and will change it to my benefit (1, 3),

b) I will try to adapt to it (7, 9).

2. When I step over a small ditch or a puddle,

a) I make my first step with my right foot (1, 3),

b) I make my first step with my left foot (7, 9).

3. When somebody I know does not greet me,

a) It upsets me; I try to recollect whether I did something wrong to him or her (1, 3),

b) I do not really care, he or she may have been simply distracted by something else (7, 9).

4. When I see that a kitchen table is a mess,

a) It spoils my appetite, I will clean up before eating (1,3),

b) I will not waste time cleaning, even though I would prefer a clear table (7,9).

III

1. Being asked to describe a city in a few sentences, I would likely write the following:

a) «Tall buildings, broad avenues with lots of cars, amusement parks» (1, 3),

b) I dislike big, noisy cities crowded with traffic, in such cities I feel absolutely lost» (7, 9).

2. My life is easier when

a) I schedule my daily activities (1, 3),

b) I do not plan in advance: something may happen that will change the situation and make all the plans useless (7, 9).

3. I can tell other people's moods

a) By slightest hints, such as expressive glances, silences, characteristic gestures, conspicuous politeness (1, 3),

b) Rather badly, and may make mistakes in my guesses (7, 9).

4. When I eat,

a) I like to savor each bite, I enjoy its taste and smell, and eat slowly (1, 3),

b) I generally think of something else, and eat quickly (7, 9).

IV

1. When speaking with strangers,

a) I easily step into the role of an amiable and sociable person (1, 3),

b) I feel uneasy being open, I have trouble with small talk and giving compliments (7,9).

2. When I fail to complete my work for reasons independent of me,

a) I feel very frustrated even when the work was boring, since I like to finish what I start (1, 3),

b) It does not bother me and I move on to a more interesting task (7, 9).

3. My mood

a) Easily changes, I can switch from joy to sadness for trifles (1,3),

b) Is rather stable, it is not easy to push me out of balance (7,9).

4. I tidy up my apartment (workplace)

a) With a feeling of satisfaction and joy (1,3),

b) Only out of necessity, but I never enjoy this task (7,9).

V

1. I like to spend time

a) At big and noisy parties (1,3),

b) In a small circle of close friends (7,9).

2. In my behavior

a) I have habits I am much attached to and regularly repeat actions (1, 3),

b) I avoid routine and often make the impression of being an unpredictable person (7, 9).

3. I am most interested in

a) Subtleties of human relations and motives of other people's actions (1, 3),

b) Machinery, technology, scientific research, theories and procedures (7, 9).

4. Small details, such as a spot on my sleeve, a loose button, etc.

a) Irritate me; I cannot leave home before adjusting my dress (1, 3),

b) Will often go unnoticed (7, 9).

VI　**1. I prefer to spend my vacations**

a) Traveling to various cities, visiting museums, theaters, etc. (1, 3),

b) At a river or a lake, in silence (7, 9)

2. I lack

a) The ability to relax; I often feel overstrained (1, 3),

b) Concentration; I prefer to relax rather than to be stressed for a long time (7, 9).

3. Recognizing the proper behavior in various social situations

a) Is easy for me (1,3),

b) Is difficult for me (7,9).

4. When I look at a piece of art work,

a) I first notice the details and then see the piece as a whole (1,3),

b) I appreciate the whole image and then begin to study details (7, 9).

VII　**1. A constant flow of new information through radio, TV, newspapers, magazines, etc.**

a) Is something I really need (1,3),

b) Makes me tired and I periodically dream of spending quiet time in the countryside away from media outlets (7,9).

2. Which is more likely to keep me up at night?

a) Loud music in my neighbor's apartment (1,3),

b) Uncomfortable bed (7,9).

3. When troubles happen in my life,

a) I go to my friends, who can emotionally support me in hard times (1, 3),

b) I retreat inside myself and deal with it on my own (7, 9).

4. I would rather have

a) One bird in my hand (1, 3),

b) Two birds in a bush (7, 9).

VIII

1. When looking for something particular at a department store,

a) I would immediately ask for assistance (1, 3),

b) I would do my best to find the item on my own before asking for help (7,9).

2. My movements are

a) Sharp and distinct rather than smooth and rounded (1, 3),

b) Smooth and rounded rather than sharp and distinct (7, 9).

3. When I hear about a tragedy in someone's life,

a) I empathize with the person, even when I do not know them (1, 3),

b) I consider the situation philosophically, as such things happen in life (7, 9).

4. As for details of landscapes, faces of newly met people, elements of clothing, etc.

a) I easily recollect them (1, 3),

b) I hardly if ever recollect them (7, 9).

IX

1. After I start a new job,

a) In a month I know everybody including colleagues from my own office and people from neighboring departments (1,3),

b) Even a year later I only know those with whom I have direct contact (7, 9).

2. I aim at

a) Planning my actions and allocating resources in advance (1, 3),

b) Not binding myself to a certain scheme and acting without a pre-scheduled plan (7, 9).

3. When one of my close friends is in trouble and very upset about it, I will try

a) To express my sympathy, provide emotional support, even when it is obvious to me that my friend is at fault (1,3),

b) To help my friend by analyzing the mistakes which brought about the situation (7,9).

4. In other people's opinion, I am

a) A sober-minded realist (1,3),

b) A daydreamer (7,9).

V **1. In a company of strangers**

a) I easily initiate a conversation and try to involve the others (1,3),

b) I wait for others to start the conversation (7,9).

2. The word that best describes my behavior is:

a) Systematic (1,3),

b) Spontaneous (7,9).

3. My level of emotion

a) Is rather high; sometimes I am so agitated that I cannot complete my work (1,3),

b) Is moderate and unlikely to intervene with my affairs (7,9).

4. When I buy something new,

a) I value it and handle it with care (1,3),

b) I may be careless with it, misplace it, or even forget I have it (7,9).

Deciphering the test

When you add up your scores in each of the 4 lines, you will get your line totals in the column XI, which may vary between 10 and 90. When your score is between 45 and 55, the respective criterion is not determined for sure; otherwise, when it exceeds 55 or is less than 45, your result is rather reliable.

Line 1:	10—45 — Extraversion	55—90 — Introversion
Line 2:	10—45 — Rationality	55—90 — Irrationality
Line 3:	10—45 — Feeling	55—90 — Thinking
Line 4:	10—45 — Sensation	55—90 — Intuition

Write in the column XII your results by each of the 4 dichotomies. Now you can find your psychological type using the Table 2.1 on page 40—41 . When you are between the two poles of any of the dichotomies, we advise you to compare your result with those of other tests concerning the same psychological trait. Anyway, determining the psychological type is not an easy task, and problems are often related to the fact that the tested do not recognize their psychological characteristics, or that they do not understand well the meaning of a particular question. In such cases we advise you to read the book more attentively, just because when people understand phrases of a psychological test too literally, without a context, their real meaning may be lost and the personality type will be determined wrongly.

Literature

1. *Аугустинавичюте А.* Соционика, т. 1, 2.— Санкт-Петербург: Terra Fantastica; Москва: «Издательство АСТ», 1998.

2. *Гуленко В., Молодцов А.* Соционика для руководителя.— Киев: Изд-во Всесоюзного заочного университета управления персоналом, 1991.

3. *Гуленко В.* Менеджмент слаженной команды.— Новосибирск: Изд-во РИПЭЛ 1995.

4. *Филатова Е.* Личность в зеркале соционики.—С.-Петербург: Б.С.К., 2001.

5. *Филатова Е.* Соционика для всех.— С.-Петербург: Б.С.К.,1999.

6. *Филатова Е.* Соционика в портретах и примерах.— Москва: Доброе слово, 2005

7. *Фрейд З.* Введение в психоанализ.— М.: Наука, 1989.

8. *Юнг К.* Психологические типы.— С.-Петербург: Ювента, Москва: Прогресс-Универс, 1995.

9. *Юнг К.* Аналитическая психология: теория и практика.— С.-Петербург: Б.С.К., 1998.

10. *Keirsey D., Bates M.* Please Understand Me.

11. *Keirsey D.* Please Understand Me II.

12. *Otto Kroeger, Janet Thuesen.* Type Talk.

13. *Otto Kroeger, Janet Thuesen.* Type Talk at Work.

14. *Otto Kroeger, Janet Thuesen.* 16 Ways to Love Your Lover.

15. *Jean M. Kummerow, Nancy D. Barger, Linda K. Kirby.* Work Types. Warner Books, A Time Isabel B. Warner Co., 1997.

16. *Betty Lou Leaver.* Teaching the Whole Class.

17. *Myers with Peter Myers.* Gifts Differing. Consulting Psychologist Press, Palo Alto, 1968.

18. *James Newman.* Psychological Theory // Bulletin of Psychological Type, 1991 (several issues).

19. *Paul Tieger, Barbara Barron-Tieger.* Do What You Are: Discover the Perfect Career for You through the Secrets of Personality Type.

20. *Paul Tieger, Barbara Barron-Tieger.* The Art of Speed Reading People.

21. *Paul Tieger, Barbara Barron-Tieger.* Nurture By Nature.

Internet

www.socioniko.net — a multilingual socionic site that uses (by author's permission) C. Filatova's pictures of people belonging to all the 16 types.

www.Socionics.us — Rick DeLong's site on Socionics.

www.Socionics.ibc.com.ua — the International Socionic Institute in Kiev, Ukraine.

www.the16types.info—probably the best English-speaking socionic forum in the Internet + some basic information about Socionics

www.Socionics.com — a site presenting a non-traditional view on Socionics as a theory of «visual identification» of people.

www.similarminds.com—non-socionic: several personality typologies (including Jungian) in comparison + forum.

CPSIA information can be obtained
at www.ICGtesting.com
Printed in the USA
LVOW04s2311181017
552969LV00013B/307/P